GANDHI'S HOPE

FAITH MEETS FAITH

An Orbis Series in Interreligious Dialogue
Paul F. Knitter & William R. Burrows, General Editors

Editorial Advisors
John Berthrong
Diana Eck
Karl-Josef Kuschel
Lamin Sanneh
George E. Tinker
Felix Wilfred

In the contemporary world, the many religions and spiritualities stand in need of greater communication and cooperation. More than ever before, they must speak to, learn from, and work with each other in order to maintain their vital identities and to contribute to fashioning a better world.

The FAITH MEETS FAITH Series seeks to promote interreligious dialogue by providing an open forum for exchange among followers of different religious paths. While the Series wants to encourage creative and bold responses to questions arising from contemporary appreciations of religious plurality, it also recognizes the multiplicity of basic perspectives concerning the methods and content of interreligious dialogue.

Although rooted in a Christian theological perspective, the Series does not limit itself to endorsing any single school of thought or approach. By making available to both the scholarly community and the general public works that represent a variety of religious and methodological viewpoints, FAITH MEETS FAITH seeks to foster an encounter among followers of the religions of the world on matters of common concern.

Faith Meets Faith Series

GANDHI'S HOPE

Learning from Other Religions as a Path to Peace

Jay McDaniel

ORBIS BOOKS
Maryknoll, New York 10545

Founded in 1970, Orbis Books endeavors to publish works that enlighten the mind, nourish the spirit, and challenge the conscience. The publishing arm of the Maryknoll Fathers and Brothers, Orbis seeks to explore the global dimensions of the Christian faith and mission, to invite dialogue with diverse cultures and religious traditions, and to serve the cause of reconciliation and peace. The books published reflect the opinions of their authors and are not meant to represent the official position of the Maryknoll Society. To obtain more information about Maryknoll and Orbis Books, please visit our website at www.maryknoll.org.

Library of Congress Cataloging-in-Publication Data

McDaniel, Jay, 1949–
  Gandhi's hope : learning from other religions as a path to peace / Jay McDaniel.
    p. cm. — (Faith meets faith)
  Includes index.
  ISBN 1-57075-590-6 (pbk.)
  1. Religions. I. Title. II. Series.
  BL80.3.M39 2003
    201'.5—dc22
                                    2004026051

Contents

Acknowledgments

One time, when trying to draw a leaf in an art class, I found myself dissatisfied with how little my own drawing resembled the actual leaf before me. The leaf seemed infinitely amazing with its shadows, shapes, and various tones of brown, green, and grey. My drawing seemed incredibly simple by contrast. The teacher came up to me and said: "Please understand that your drawing does not need to look like that leaf. It is your drawing with its own tone and texture. Just let it be what it is. But also know that the very act of drawing is a collaborative process. You've not been drawing alone." I asked her who I was collaborating with as I drew, and she said, "The paper and pen, of course, but still more deeply the leaf. Nature is inherently creative, and in drawing your own leaf, you are adding in a very small way to its creativity."

Writing this book feels like drawing that leaf. I have been surrounded by people of many different religions who have inspired me with their sincerity, depth, wisdom, and creativity. I know that their lives and wisdom far transcend the simple generalizations I draw in this book and also that they would not agree with all of the ideas I propose. Still, I am tremendously indebted to them. They include Imam Islam Mosaad and Mrs. Wendy Moursi from the Islamic Society of Arkansas; Zen Master Keido Fukushima and Dr. Jeff Shore from Kyoto, Japan; Dr. Malay Muzumdar from the Hindu community in Little Rock; and Rabbi Eugene Levy from Temple B'Nai Israel in Little Rock. If peace between religions means friendship between religions, these individuals are among the friends who have inspired one or another of the ideas in this book.

I also want to thank friends at Hendrix College, where I have been teaching world religions for many years. These friends include colleagues in the Department of Religion, John Farthing, Frances Flannery-Dailey, and Jane Harris, and also many students in numerous sections of "Religion in a Global Context" and "State of the World." It would be impossible to name all of these students, but four deserve special mention, since they helped critique early drafts of the book: Amelia Cates, Joni Podschun, Katie Whitney, and Bekka Sappington. Each of them offered ideas that helped frame this book and also helped me avoid countless grammatical infelicities.

Finally, I want to thank members of several Christian communities with whom I shared parts of the book. When I speak of a kind of Christianity that has "deep listening" as part of its very essence, I speak of something I have witnessed quite often. The listeners include members of the Dialogue Class and the Seeking More Light Class of the Second Presbyterian Church in Little Rock; members of the Forum Class at the First United Methodist Church in Conway, Arkansas, especially but not exclusively Jim Beal, Lamar Davis, and Austin Glenn; participants in the Journey into Silence Meditation group at St. Peter's Episcopal Church in Conway, Arkansas; and sisters at Mount Saint Benedict Monastery in Erie, Pennsylvania. One of the sisters, a woman in her late eighties, said to me: "You know, we Christians need people of other religions in order to be complete. It's the differences that make life so beautiful. I'm glad Gandhi was a Hindu!" As she spoke, I found myself thinking, "Yes, and sometimes it's the similarities, too. If following Christ means being someone with a heart as wide as yours, I want to be a Christian, too." I am grateful to all these people for making this book possible.

Introduction

> *I can see clearly the time coming when*
> *people belonging to different faiths will*
> *have the same regard for other faiths that*
> *they have for their own.*
>
> —Mahatma Gandhi

This small book is written for the spiritually interested general reader who would like to learn about and from the world religions; who is troubled by the arrogance and violence that can sometimes be inflicted on the world in the name of religion; who believes that despite their shortcomings all religions embody wisdom that is essential to the well-being of life; and who is especially interested in prospects for peace between religions. I hope that the book might prove helpful not only to individual readers who are affiliated with one or another of the world religions but also to those who think of themselves as "spiritually interested but not religiously affiliated." I hope the book might also be useful to groups of people who are actively engaged in interreligious dialogue in the context of local, multireligious communities or who, while not actively involved in dialogue, are engaged in a sympathetic study of the world religions in the context of a college classroom or community of faith. I believe that a study of the religions—if done with a desire to learn *from* the religions and not simply about them—is itself an act of peacemaking. It helps create that culture of generosity and hospitality, that culture of peace, which is the only real hope for the world.

Given this need for a culture of peace, we best begin our deliberations with one of the most influential peacemakers of the past century: Mahatma Gandhi. Was he right? *Will* there come a time when people belonging to different faiths will have the same regard for other faiths that they have for their own?

Perhaps not. The rise of religious fundamentalism throughout the world—especially among the world's two most populous religions, Christianity and Islam—can suggest that the future will be filled with tension and conflict, violence and hatred. Some people say that there will not be a harmony of religions but rather a clash of civilizations in which religious divisions will be paramount. And some even hope for this conflict, seeing it as a precursor to the judgment day when all except the true believers will be consigned to hell. Let us be honest. Gandhi may have been very naive.

And yet there are small signs of hope, often in surprising places. Consider the local bookstore. When we walk into the bookstore and turn to the section called religion, we find beautifully illustrated religious texts from around the world: the Bhagavad-Gita from Hinduism, the Tao te Ching from Taoism, the Dhammapada from Buddhism, the Zohar from Judaism, the Qur'an of Islam. If we ask the bookseller how these books are selling, we often discover that they are selling as well as, if not better than, the Bible. If we look a little further, we find countless commentaries on these books written by gifted authors who bring the traditions to life for the spiritually interested general reader. The study of world religions is not merely the pastime of the scholars in the university; it is also the passion of seekers on the street. These seekers are not interested in a clash of civilizations; they are interested in learning from the many religions. They hope that, despite the numerous failings of the historical world religions, each contains wisdom conducive to a flourishing of life.

Some of these seekers define themselves as "spiritual but not religious." Their critics often accuse them of adopting a consumerist approach to the world religions. "You are shopping for religion like people shop at Wal-Mart," the critics say, "and you are failing to honor the depth and integrity of the religions you are considering." There may be truth in this criticism. The religions are not like toothpaste, and we do them a disservice by pretending we can simply paste a little on. But Gandhi himself was a creative eclectic of sorts, taking wisdom from Christianity and Jainism and Islam, all the while understanding himself as a good Hindu. He had roots as well as wings. Perhaps some who define themselves as "spiritual but not religious" are simply trying to say, along with Gandhi, that truths are many and all make the whole richer. As they see things, it would be blasphemous not to honor truth wherever it is found. It would be to pretend that truth is the private possession of one and only one group.

Moreover, some among the seekers will be religiously affiliated themselves. They will define themselves as "both religious and spiritual," meaning that they belong to a particular religious communion—Jewish or Christian or Muslim or Buddhist—and that their roots in this community give them wings to fly in openness to other traditions. They will see being religious as a journey, and they will open the pages of the various books at the bookstore not despite their religious affiliation but because of it. As a Muslim friend once put it to me: "Being a Muslim does not mean having all the truth; it means being free to pursue the truth, trustful that it is of God and from God. Openness to other traditions is part of the journey. Islam teaches that a prophet has been sent to every nation. I'm interested in what the other prophets have to say."

All of this suggests that, even with the rise of fundamentalisms the world over, there may be seeds of hope. There may be a small but growing core of people whose hearts feel called not simply to security and certainty but still more deeply to openness and pilgrimage. Part of this pilgrimage can and should involve openness to people of the many different religions and a delight in religious diversity itself.

Of course, religious diversity is not new. Scholars disagree on how religion began, but it seems probable that the many religions began in differentiated form because from their beginnings human cultures developed in many parts of the world. We can safely assume that as long as there have been *any* religions in the world, there have been *many* religions. Equally important, a consciousness of this diversity is not new. In many parts of the world, people of different religions have been living in proximity to each other, sometimes peacefully and sometimes in conflict, for a very long time. Modern people are not the first to realize that they—we—are one among many.

What *is* new, though, is the degree and scope of this awareness. Through information gained from books and movies, television and the internet, newspapers and magazines, something new is happening. There is an explosion of information about the world religions, some of it reliable and some of it not, and parallel to this explosion there is an increased interest in these faiths and traditions. As a result, *more* people are *more* aware of the world religions than at any time in the past, and this awareness is a growing part of the collective consciousness of the whole of humanity.

In many places in the world, this growing awareness is matched by a need for new kinds of community. Many urban centers are now microcosms of global religious diversity, and this fact presents a challenge and an opportunity. Consider the findings of Diana Eck's *A New Religious America: How a Christian Country Became the World's Most Religiously Diverse Nation*. Fifteen years ago, Eck started sending graduate students from Harvard into various parts of the United States to explore the diversity of their home regions, and she began to realize, along with the students, that there is more diversity in the United States than anyone had quite realized. There are more Muslims in the United States than Presbyterians, and Los Angeles is home to more kinds of Buddhism than any other city in the world. According to Eck, the United States is now the most religiously diverse nation on the planet. This new level of American religious diversity is historically important: "The fate of a vibrant pluralism in the United States will have an important impact on the fate of religious pluralism worldwide," because citizens of the United States are a living experiment in how much pluralism a nation can tolerate and enjoy.[1]

This book emerges in the larger context of Eck's challenge. I want to suggest that human beings can tolerate and enjoy a great deal of pluralism, perhaps more than many of us have yet imagined; and I offer a constructive theology of world religions which encourages such tolerance and enjoyment. In some ways I offer what might best be called a *Christian* theology of world religions, because the book is shaped by my own Christian faith. Still, the book is not written for Christians alone. I write for people of many religions and no religion who, like me, want to learn about and from the many religions.

As a Christian, I draw part of my inspiration for welcoming religious diversity from the Benedictine tradition. The Benedictines teach that whenever a stranger comes to the gates of the monastery, that stranger should be welcomed as Christ, even if the stranger is Muslim or Jewish, Hindu or agnostic, Buddhist or atheist. Welcoming the stranger as Christ does not mean thinking about Jesus rather than the stranger. Rather, it means being present to the stranger, listening with a sympathetic and caring ear and with a willingness to honor the wisdom the stranger brings. As Paul puts it in the Bible, love is patient and forgiving and does not insist on its own way (1 Cor 13:4). The Benedictines also add that the person doing the welcoming—even if that person is simply a guest in the monastery—embodies the very spirit of Christ, whether or not she herself happens to be Christian. Whenever we see hospitality, we see the spirit of Christ, thus named or not. The good news, therefore, is that the spirit of Christ is not reducible to Christians. Christ is more than Christianity.

As a Christian, I have often sensed this spirit in Gandhi. Just as Jesus belongs to the whole world and not just to Christians, Gandhi belongs to the whole world and not just to Hindus. It is no accident, then, that part of the inspiration for the theme of this book comes from Gandhi, whose commitments to non-violence and openness to many religions stretch the Christian imagination in needed directions. Gandhi believed that the world will never and need never have a single religion. He hoped for a time when people of different religions will be secure in their faith and yet open to learning from others in a spirit of friendship. As a Christian, I hope for the same state of affairs. I hope for a world in which there are many religions, Christianity among them. It seems to me that the emergence of non-violent, multi-religious communities is one sign of what things may look like when the will of God is done "on earth as it is in heaven."

Therefore, one of my purposes in this book is to promote peace between religions, understood as friendship-in-community and friendship-at-a-distance. Friendship-in-community can be seen as people of different religions traveling in the same buses; sharing the same workplaces; enjoying together various kinds of recreation, such as music and sports; and working together to build communities that are socially just, ecologically sustainable, and spiritually satisfying for all. A good image for this would be that of two people from different religions extending the hand of friendship to one another.

Ideally both sides extend the hand of friendship simultaneously. However, in some circumstances, the best way to extend a hand of friendship is to withdraw the hand of domination. This is especially important in situations where religious minorities feel, and sometimes are, overwhelmed by religious majorities such that the minorities simply seek to practice their religion without interference. In these instances, the majority can extend the hand of friendship by withdrawing the hand of domination and by encouraging, in a non-controlling way, the practice of the other religion. In the United States, for example, Christians can and should do this with Native Americans, by helping them to protect their sacred lands from commercial use. In Iran, to offer another example, Muslims can and should do this for Jews, Christians, and others who sometimes feel inhibited from practicing their faith. Friendship begins with creative encouragement, one aspect of which is simply "letting be."

However, it need not end there. In the context of local communities, there can be an evolution of friendship, just as there are developmental stages in any community. Friendship begins with respect on the part of religious majorities for religious minorities, assuring that the minority's rights to practice its religion are protected. It can evolve into mutual interaction, through which people share in work and pleasure, trustful that their differences add spice to life. And it can then grow into mutual transformation, through which members of different religions learn from one another, each transformed by the wisdom of the other. Thus there are the three successive stages of interreligious dialogue in local communities: respect, mutual interaction, and mutual transformation.

It is important to recognize, though, that friendship between religions is more than friendship in local communities. It is also an attitude of mind or heart through which religiously minded people feel inwardly disposed to welcome people of other religions—to honor their wisdom—even if those others live in other parts of the state, other parts of the nation, or other parts of the world. In an age of electronic globalization, where people from many cultures and religions are gathered together in a single web of communication, this second and more general appreciation of the many world religions is as important as friendship-in-community. It is friendship-at-a-distance, and it helps create a climate of trust and respect, which can help shape decisions made by media, governments, and corporations.

Both forms of peace between religions—friendship-in-community and friendship-at-a-distance—require humility. They require an inner recognition that truth is always more than any person's experience of it and any religion's experience of it. Indeed, they require what Gandhi called "friendly readings" of other religions, according to his grandson Arun Gandhi in a lecture given at Hendrix College on October 23, 2002. Thus a religiously minded person approaches another tradition not only with an interest in its failings and faults but also with an appreciation of its wisdom, no matter how unfamiliar the other tradition may seem. This appreciation is best cultivated by an emotional sensitivity that runs deeper than simple interest. We might call it delight in diversity. From the perspective of this book, delight in diversity is a diagnostic test of authentic spirituality. God is not One-over-many but rather One-embracing-many, and we cannot embrace God without embracing the many whom God embraces.[2] The many include plants and animals, hills and rivers, trees and stars, and they include people of the many cultures and religions. Without delight in manyness, we cannot live as one with each other. There can be no peace.

For some people, however, the word "peace" has somewhat boring connotations. It suggests a state of affairs that is non-violent and harmonious but not necessarily intense or surprising. In this book, I will try to define peace more creatively, proposing that peace at its deepest level has a musical quality like that of an improvisational jazz concert. The music at such a concert consists of a creative and evolving harmony of sound produced by different musicians who have the material wherewithal to purchase their instruments and who are cooperatively responding to one another in an ongoing live performance, often in surprising and joyful ways. If the concert is to continue, the musicians must be willing to keep on playing even when things threaten to fall apart, and they must be willing to forgive one another for the mistakes they might make. Peace is like this. It can be unpredictable, filled with creative tensions, and it can have its sad and mournful moments. But it is cooperative and creative, surprising and sometimes joyful, and its competitive dimensions do not degenerate into violence.

Equally important, peace requires listening to the silences between the sounds, because it is the silences that give the sounds their meaning. In communities that embody peace, the silences are the things that people cannot say or have not yet said but that are part of their deeper intentions and hopes. In peace at its deepest and best level, then, the participants who create peace listen for these silences and handle them with respect. The spiritual foundation of peace does not lie simply in a capacity to make peace and build communities that are just and sustainable; it lies also in listening sympathetically and deeply to the subjective aims of others, responding in ways that are new, surprising, and beautiful. In the beginning is the listening, and this listening is with God and is God.

In the interests of a creative peace, then, I have three specific aims in this book. First, as already explained, I want to offer a theological companion to the study of world religions that might help people undertake critical yet friendly readings of the world religions. It is not itself a study of the world religions, but rather something that might be useful for people who are already engaged in such a study, formally or informally. I must emphasize at the outset that this book is interpretive and selective. I treat but a few of the many insights offered by the various world religions, and I interpret those insights as I treat them. I can only hope that some of my interpretations might be helpful.

One thing unique about the approach I recommend is that it emphasizes *complementary pluralism*. Complementary pluralism is the view that the insights of the many religions are different but complementary, such that no religion contains all the truth even as all contain some of the truth. At the heart of complementary pluralism is the assumption that there is more wisdom in all the religions taken together than in any of them considered alone, and that people of different religions have much to learn from each other, because insights from one religion help complete and correct insights from the others.

The opposite of complementary pluralism is *identist pluralism*. Identist pluralism is the view that the insights of the many religions are identical, such that any given religion contains all the truth relevant to human flourishing, and one need not turn to the others. Advocates of identist pluralism sometimes appeal to the image of a single mountaintop to which all spiritual seekers aspire, albeit calling it by different names such as "Brahman" or "God" or "Allah" or "the Mystery." The general idea is that even as one group might be using one set of equipment to climb the mountain, namely the teachings and practices of its own tradition, others are using other sets of equipment that are equally valid for them. Hence, the goals of all the religions would be identical.

There is wisdom in this identist point of view, since sometimes various religions do indeed have common aims and goals. Such commonalities are to be celebrated; recognition of identical goals can help bring about peace between religions. But the mountaintop image also carries liabilities. If we are strong in our own convictions concerning what is ultimate, we can too easily imagine the top of the mountain in terms that are familiar to us and thus project onto others our own aims and goals even as those others might have different aims and goals. We can fail to appreciate the differences.

As an alternative to the mountaintop image, I suggest that of a rainbow, proposing that the religious traditions can have different aims and goals but that these differences can be complementary rather than contradictory, as are colors in a rainbow. What a Buddhist means by "awakening to the interconnectedness of all things" may not be what a Christian means by "trust in God." It would be a mistake to say that they are climbing the same mountain. Still, it may be true that "awakening to interconnectedness" and "trust in God" can co-exist in a person's life and that each can be enriched by the other, especially if God is understood as a supreme expression of interconnectedness rather than a supreme exception to it. The guiding ideal of this book is not that the truth is one while the paths are many. Instead, it is that the truths are many, and all make the whole richer. Still more precisely, it is that the insights of the many traditions are manifold, that sometimes these insights are identical and sometimes they are different, but that all of the insights make the whole of life richer.

Here the phrase "whole of life" means several things. It means the whole of human life insofar as the insights help humans live more wisely and compassionately in daily life. It means the whole of biological life insofar as at least some of the insights, when translated into practice, help humans to live in greater mutuality with other living beings. And it means the whole of the divine life insofar as the divine life itself is One who embraces the many and is enriched by the many thus embraced. There are wholes within wholes, communities within communities. God is the sacred whole—the most inclusive environment—within whom all wholes subsist.

For people interested in learning from the religions, the question quickly becomes: "What aspects of those traditions should I turn my attention to?" If turning to other religions is like walking into a forest on a dark night with a flashlight in our hands, what should we be looking for as we cast our beam in one direction and then another?

Often people begin by looking to the verbalized teachings of the religions. This is especially true for Christian-influenced students, who naturally think that other religions may first and foremost be about "right belief," since many forms of Christianity emphasize belief as a defining characteristic of authentic Christianity. However, I believe that focusing primarily on belief is a mistake. I propose that the insights of the various religions emerge from at least two forms of learning: (1) learning from "mind to body" as it occurs in reading sacred texts and the passing on of verbal teachings and (2) learning from "body to mind" as evidenced in meditation, ritual, and concrete acts of love. I propose also that the insights acquired from "mind to body" or "body to mind" can themselves take the forms of truthful belief, truthful awareness, and truthful living. If we are Christian, for example, truthful belief would lie in saying and believing that God is love; truthful awareness would lie in empathizing with the feelings of others, thereby loving them in our hearts; and truthful living would lie in responding to their needs with compassion. Even in Christianity, it seems to me, truthful awareness and truthful living are ultimately more important than truthful belief. Indeed, truthful belief, if isolated from the other two forms of truth, too easily lapses into sloganeering, where slogans concerning "God" and "love" come to replace practicing the presence of God in daily life. My more general point, though, is not for Christians alone. It is for anyone studying the religions with an eye to learning from them. We will miss the wisdom of religion if we think its truths are limited to matters of belief. Sometimes we learn more from a religion by seeing how its participants dance or pray, sing or serve, than by asking what they believe.

To summarize: the first aim of this book is to offer an interpretive companion for the study of world religions. The approach taken is one of complementary pluralism as a way of thinking about the religions and helping religiously affiliated readers *live* from the truths of their own tradition and simultaneously *learn* from the truths of other traditions in ways that add new insights to their lives. The rainbow analogy is most appropriate for the tone of this book. The British essayist John Ruskin once said that the purest of minds are those that love colors the most.[3] I hope this book helps readers appreciate different colors.

My second aim is related to the first but turns in a more sobering direction. It is to speak honestly about problems of religious violence and intolerance, suggesting that, even as religious traditions contain wisdom conducive to the flourishing of life, they also contain foolishness that can lend itself to tragedy. Sometimes in making these more negative claims, we are tempted to say that the religions themselves are not the problem; it is instead the people who practice them. This is not my approach. I think that religions can be part of the problem insofar as they contain teachings and practices that can lend themselves to violence and prejudice, arrogance and ignorance. This fact—the fact that religions can be evil—does not contradict the fact that religions can also be good. Religions are like people: mixed bags. If we are affiliated with a particular religion, we do not need to think that our religion—or any other religion for that matter—is perfect in order to find meaning in it. When religions are elevated to the status of perfection, they are divinized and made into idols. Then religion becomes an object of devotion in itself; Christianity becomes Christianism. Conscious of this possibility, religious people need to recognize that just as we can grow and change over time, sometimes for the better, religions can also grow and change over time, sometimes for the better. Just as there can be progress in science, with new views replacing old views over time, there can be progress in religion as well.

My third aim is to offer some guidelines for interreligious dialogue that might follow from the recognition that religions can be both wise and foolish. Often when people speak of dialogue they have in mind interchange for the sake of mutual understanding and acceptance. Of course, this is a worthy and much-needed goal. We need mutual understanding in our world.

But, as noted above in discussing friendship, another purpose of dialogue can be mutual transformation, in which the dialogue itself changes participants in different traditions, not in ways that lead them to abandon their religion but in ways that enable them to grow in their religion. Such dialogue can include honest and sincere disagreement as well as agreement; it can include mutual criticism as well as mutual appreciation. A Christian can learn from Buddhists, for example, in ways that help make her a better Christian, and a Buddhist can learn from Christians in ways that help make him a better Buddhist. Not simply mutual understanding, then, but mutual transformation can be the aim of dialogue.

The reality and possibility of transformation points to a certain hope I offer in this book. It is that religiously affiliated people—Christians and Muslims and Buddhists and Jews—can entertain the *potential desirability* of a hybrid religious identity in which, even as a person is primarily rooted in one religious tradition, she can be secondarily rooted in others, to the end of becoming more fully human. I am myself a Christian of this kind. I am a Christian and also a professor of world religions, and as a Christian I am deeply influenced by the many world religions that I have taught over the years.

Of course, all of us are already hybrids many times over in the actual living of our lives. Every relationship we have with anyone becomes part of our ongoing history such that, in the language of the philosopher Alfred North Whitehead, whom I will introduce shortly, we are never simply one thing but always already many things. We are always already, to use Whitehead's words, a process of "the many becoming one."[4] Nevertheless, many people in the Abrahamic family of religions fear hybridity when it comes to religion, because it can seem to dilute religious life. And sometimes, of course, it can. Whether hybridity is desirable must be determined on a case-by-case basis. For some people in some situations, exclusive rootedness in a single religious tradition is the preferred option.

Sometimes, however, advocates of exclusive rootedness can forget that no human being—and in fact no religion—is an island. They can criticize hybridity as unhealthy eclecticism, forgetting that every religion in the world has evolved, and continues to evolve, by assimilating insights and practices that were alien to predecessors in the tradition. No religion stands on its own with boundaries totally immune from external influences. All religions undergo ongoing and evolving development. Sometimes this development can take the form of creative synthesis, in which previously unknown insights are added to a tradition, changing the tradition in the process. What is said of religions can also be said of individuals and communities. All can change over time by learning from others.

It is important, then, to distinguish between creative synthesis, in which a person appropriates insights from other paths in a respectful way, and unhealthy eclecticism, in which a person appropriates insights from another path in a disrespectful and shallow way, without tasting the depths of the tradition thus appropriated. I want to recommend that, for some people in some circumstances, creative synthesis is itself a form of religious living. It is healthy eclecticism.

It might seem as if creative synthesis is more of an option for non-theists than for theists, especially if the latter appeal to special revelation. When a Christian appeals to God's special revelation in Jesus, for example, or a Muslim to God's special revelation in the Qur'an, it is very tempting to assume that there is nothing important to learn from any other source. In this book, however, I suggest the contrary. Drawing from various strands of the New Testament and the Qur'an, many Christians and Muslims believe that God is within the whole of creation as a lure toward wisdom in the heart of each human being. If God is omnipresent in this way, it would be odd and perhaps even sinful to reject revelation from unfamiliar places in the name of maintaining a solid identity within one tradition. It would seem to be more honest, perhaps even more faithful, to be open to diversity, trustful that, even as one has received special revelation from God, God is always more than one's experience of God.

Of course, the three aims that I have just identified are quite bold and they are riddled with theological and philosophical assumptions that require defense. Moreover, achieving the three aims could easily take many thousands of pages, and given the shortness of this book and the limitations of my own abilities, I will be fortunate if I achieve even a small portion of them. In some ways, I am offering food for thought upon which I hope others might build not only by appreciating the ideas but also by criticizing them. In any case, one thing is clear. There can be no neutral, a-historical, value-free place to make the proposals I will be making. In this book, therefore, I will be speaking from a particular religious and philosophical point of view that is based on process theology.

Process theology is a form of theology that emerged in the 1930s at the University of Chicago and that was influenced by the philosophy of Alfred North Whitehead. Most of the advocates of process theology are Christian, but some are also Jewish, Hindu, Buddhist, Bahai, and Muslim. What they appreciate about Whitehead is that he offers a way of appreciating so many different kinds of religious sensibilities. I will be introducing process theology in the first chapter, but for now let me explain why it is important to me.

This book has roots in two roles I play in life. One is that of a college teacher of world religions who has spent a great deal of time learning from the religions and from my students. Over the years I have found process theology especially helpful in learning about and from the religions. This leads me to believe that process theology can be a helpful companion for people of many religions and of no religion as they seek to learn about and from the world religions. Learning of this sort contributes a climate of peace between religions. This is why education about the world's religions is central to a more peaceful world. Whiteheadian or process theology can assist in this education.

The other role is that of a practicing Christian who has been actively involved for many years in Christian-Muslim and Christian-Buddhist dialogue. Here, too, I find that process theology can be helpful in enabling Christians to appreciate and learn from the core wisdom of other religions, thus enriching Christian life, even as Christians simultaneously recognize that they—we—have wisdom to share with people of other religions.

From a process perspective, the heart of Christian wisdom does not only lie simply in proclaiming exclusively "Christian" insights that determine Christian turf but also, and more important, in listening itself and in being willing to be converted, again and again, by the healing wisdom of others insofar as it is conducive to love. This kind of listening is part of that always-arriving-but-never-fully-arrived community of love that was the center of Jesus' concern. The idea that Christian wisdom includes listening has important implications for Christian theology. It means that Christian theology need not always be about "Christianity." It can be about Buddhism and Islam, Hinduism and Taoism, Judaism and Jainism, and a host of other perspectives as well, insofar as they are conducive to love. The vocation of the Christian is not to protect Christian identity for its own sake; it is to be an extension of Jesus' healing ministry. In the context of religious pluralism, deep listening accompanied by compassionate response is an essential dimension of this extension.

This book has three chapters and a conclusion. Each chapter is divided into numerous sections that are, in their own way, mini-essays. The book does not proceed linearly but rather radially, circling various subjects, sometimes again and again, from different angles. Perhaps the book is best imagined as a mandala with the myriad topics treated in the sections as images within the larger whole. These images include pleasant subjects like "peace" and "truth" and "salvation" and "ultimate reality" and "God" and less pleasant subjects like "sin" and "violence" and a consideration of what happens "when religion becomes evil." I hope that, by the time you have completed this book, you will understand a process approach to each of these subjects that can then help you make peace in the global village. Without peace between religions, there can be no peace in the world. May this book, in some small way, serve that larger and much more important end.

1

Let a Thousand Flowers Bloom
Process Theology and the World Religions

> *Hope is the thing with feathers*
> *That perches in the soul,*
> *And sings the tune without the words,*
> *And never stops at all.*
>
> —Emily Dickinson

Our concern is with peace between religions. I borrow the title of this chapter from a man who was not very peaceful and not very religious: Mao Zedong. In the 1960s Mao said "Let a thousand flowers bloom" as a way of encouraging Chinese to be open to ideas from many sources during the Cultural Revolution. Students of history know that the chairman did not follow his own advice, and many Chinese were persecuted and killed. I do not use the phrase to legitimize this tragedy.

Instead, I use it more hopefully, in the same spirit that my wife used it some years ago as we were taking a walk one morning. We came upon a grassy plain and she took note of the many different kinds of flowers that were blossoming in a patch of grass: Black-Eyed Susans, Queen Anne's Lace, Buttercups, Wild Peas, Crimson Clovers, Wild Roses, Purple Vetches, and White Toothworts. Not exactly a thousand flowers, but enough to make the small area a gorgeous splash of color. "Let a thousand flowers bloom," she said. And I thought to myself, "And let a thousand religions bloom, too." I was expressing the hope—indeed the prayer—that the world's religions at their non-violent and non-arrogant best might form a collective splash of color that adds richness to the world and its encircling mystery, God.

There is, of course, a problem. The world's religions are not always at their non-violent and non-arrogant best. Sometimes they can exhibit weed-like properties, choking out life within and beyond their respective communities. It goes without saying that many Christians fall into this camp. Too often we Christians assume that, in the best of all worlds, there would be one and only one religion—namely, our own. In the name of our highest ideals, we fail to listen to others.

This un-listening is one example of what I mean by arrogance. It carries within it a hidden form of psychological violence because it divides the world into believers and unbelievers and then seeks to conquer that world through conversion without truly listening to the wisdom of those being converted. It assumes that Christians and Christians alone have good news.

When attitudes like this emerge within the religions, then the religious traditions—or at least the people who embody them—exemplify the very problem that got the best of Chairman Mao. We are inwardly driven by a need for control and domination, all in the name of what is "good" and "right" and "true." This need for control is combined with a desire for vindication, for proving that we have been "right" and others have been "wrong." What is necessary today, then, is a world in which religiously minded people can repent of our impulses to control others in the name of one truth, who can say along with my wife, "Let a thousand flowers bloom."

If this appeal to my wife seems too idiosyncratic, let me appeal to a more public and globally recognized figure. In the past one hundred years, the most visible advocate of a non-violent blossoming of many religions was Mahatma Gandhi. His passion in life was to help build multi-religious, self-reliant communities that were socially just, ecologically wise, and spiritually satisfying for all. This passion prefigured the hopes that many people rightly have for the world today. Gandhi did not develop a systematic theology of world religions; instead, he offered sayings in various speeches during his lifetime that illustrate a general approach.[1] Here are two examples:

> Personally I think the world as a whole will never have, and need not have, a single religion.

> For me the principal religions are equal in the sense that they are all true. They are supplying a felt want in the spiritual progress of humanity.

And here is a third example (quoted at the beginning of the introdution to this book):

> I can see clearly the time coming when people belonging to different faiths will have the same regard for other faiths that they have for their own.

These statements reflect a deep respect not only for people of different religions but also for the religions themselves. Gandhi knew, however, that if religions are to be sources of goodness in the world, they must be capable of growing and changing over time.

> Every living faith must have within itself the power of rejuvenation if it is to live.

> If we are imperfect ourselves, religion as conceived by us must also be imperfect.... Religion, being thus imperfect, is always subject to a process of evolution and reinterpretation.

All these sayings are idealistic. It is idealistic to think that religious people can embrace religious diversity, accepting themselves as one-among-many rather than one-over-many. And it is idealistic to think that they can acknowledge limitations of their inherited traditions and thus accept the possibility that there can be progress in religion.

Given this idealism, it is important to emphasize that Gandhi did not forge his beliefs in a vacuum. His considerations on peace between religions emerged in the context of his own non-violent struggles for peace in South Africa and then in India, and he was fully aware of the violence that people can inflict on one another in the name of religion. He himself died at the hands of a Hindu nationalist. Given his awareness of violence and arrogance within religions, it is all the more remarkable that he trusted that all religions also contain wisdom conducive to peace, even amid their tendencies toward violence. And it is noteworthy that, in the daily worship services of his ashram, he put this trust into practice. He encouraged reading from many of the world's scriptures, confident that, at the deepest level, the core insights of the religions are part of a larger whole—a deeper Truth—that humans rightly pursue throughout their lives and never claim fully to possess. He used the term "God" to name this deeper Truth. In Gandhi's words: "I think it is wrong to expect certainties in this world where all else but God that is Truth is an uncertainty."[2]

Gandhi's approach to religion captures the spirit of the approach I will be taking in this book. I propose that each human being possesses an indwelling lure toward truth that enables him or her to discover resources for human fulfillment. I also propose that the world's religions, when weaned of impulses toward arrogance, violence, prejudice, and ignorance, are vessels of this truth. Admittedly, I cannot quite be as optimistic as Gandhi. I cannot *see clearly* a time when people of different religions will have the same regard for other faiths that they have for their own. The forces of religious fundamentalism seem very powerful in our time, even within my own Christian tradition. But I certainly hope for a time when people will live in multi-religious communities and when their hearts and minds will be gladdened by the fact that there are many religions rather than one. And I know from personal experience as a Christian that I find things in other religions that seem lacking in my own, such that I have as much respect for them as for my own. One of these things, so vividly expressed in Gandhi's kind of Hinduism, is a respect for diversity. I cannot help but think that Christ calls Christians today into this kind of respect and that <u>Gandhi was, in his way,</u> a prophetic witness for a <u>transformation of Christian</u> consciousness. Let us briefly consider the bigger picture.

THE FIVE CHALLENGES
FACED BY THE WORLD'S RELIGIONS

Every age has its calling. In our time—the early decades of the twenty-first century—some aspects of this calling are matters of life and death. Witness the disparities between rich and poor in our world, the tragedies of war and violence, and the gradual depletion of the earth's non-renewable resources. Witness the myriad ways in which humans have not yet learned to live gently with each other or lightly on the earth. <u>In the long run it may not matter whether we are Christian or Muslim, Jewish or Buddhist,</u> Confucian or Taoist, Navaho or Cherokee. <u>What matters is that we respond to five challenges that, taken together, constitute the great work</u> of our time. They are:

To live compassionately: that is, to identify resources within our traditions that are conducive to respect and care for the community of life and to live from them, thus helping to build multi-religious communities that are just, sustainable, participatory, and non-violent

To live self-critically: that is, to acknowledge tendencies within our traditions that lend themselves to arrogance, prejudice, violence, and ignorance, to repent for them, and to add new chapters to our religion's history

To live simply: that is, to present a viable and joyful alternative to the dominant religion of our age, namely consumerism, by living simply and frugally, thereby avoiding the tragedies of poverty and the arrogance of affluence

To live ecologically: that is, to recognize that we humans are creatures among creatures on a small but magnificent planet who have ethical responsibilities to other living beings and to the whole of life

To welcome religious diversity: that is, to promote peace between religions by befriending people of other religions, trustful that the truths of the world religions are manifold, all making the whole richer

With the exception of the second challenge, which applies to people who are religiously affiliated, these challenges are applicable to a wide range of people, including people without religious affiliation. The focus here, though, is on their relevance to people with such affiliations. To the degree that religiously affiliated people respond to these challenges, there will be hope for the world, and religion will be part of the solution. And to the degree that they do not, there will be tragedy in the world, and religion will be part of the problem.

I recognize that the very word "religion" is a Western word that has been carelessly applied to the many ways of living that have evolved on our planet. Its meaning is problematic if aligned with belief in God or concern for an afterlife. Some religions—Theravada Buddhism, for example—do not involve belief in God, and many, such as Judaism and liberal Christianity, are not overly preoccupied with what happens after death. For convenience, let us simply use the word "religion" to name ways of living in the world that help gather together the myriad strands of a person's life into a single and dynamic whole. A religion is a path or a way. (In this sense, consumerism itself can be a religion, albeit an unhealthy one by my standards.) And let us recognize that the very word "religion," even as defined along these lines, is an abstraction from the many people who try to walk the way and *personal religion* [handwritten annotation]

follow the path. At some level, there are as many religions as there are people. We see these religions in the faces of young and old, women and men, Africans, Asians, Americans, and Aborigines. Almost always, the religions are not static or fully defined but rather religions-in-the-making, lived by people who are struggling to find peace of mind and beauty in their lives. There seems to be a longing within the human heart for wisdom, compassion, and freedom. That longing is religion in its deepest sense.

However, because none of us can keep track of all these six billion religions as practiced by individuals across the globe, we naturally and rightly divide them into general groupings, calling them Buddhism and Hinduism and Christianity and Islam. In this book, it is these groupings that I have in mind when I say "religion." Unless specified otherwise, then, I do not mean the individual quest for wholeness, and I do not mean consumerism. Rather, I mean the communal and institutionalized ways of living discussed by departments of religious studies in colleges and universities. The idea that these religions face five challenges is shorthand for saying that the people who belong to these groupings, by either birth or choice, face five challenges upon which the future of the world depends.

Of course, these challenges will be more difficult for some religious people than for others. It may be easier for indigenous peoples to recognize kinship with other creatures than for more anthropocentric Muslims, Jews, and Christians. Equally important, not all of the challenges are relevant to all people. Consider the challenge to live simply. This challenge is most relevant to the one-fifth of the world's population who consume more than half the world's resources, depleting the world's non-renewable resources and living in a way people in the rest of the world could not possibly emulate. It is estimated that, if the whole world lived as the average American does, it would take six planets the size of the earth to supply all the resources. It is the affluent who are called to live more simply so that the poor can simply live. When considered in relation to concrete circumstances, the five challenges are on a sliding scale of perceived need and objective urgency.

relativity of obligation or responsibility [handwritten annotation]

Nevertheless, for many readers of this book—as for me—the five challenges are all relevant and *challenging*. We are called to live compassionately even if compassion makes us feel vulnerable; to live self-critically even if we are afraid of change and find it easier to criticize others than to criticize ourselves; to reject a lifestyle based on appearance, affluence, and marketable achievement even if we are deeply absorbed in it and gain from it; to recognize that we are kin to other creatures even if we prefer to think of ourselves as set apart and special; and to welcome religious diversity even if we are initially fearful of strangers and what they might teach us. And what calls? Some would say "God" and some would say "the demands of the present historical situation" and some would say "the song of the universe." Emily Dickinson would say the small bird—the thing with feathers—that perches in the soul and sings a wordless tune of hope.

Perhaps Emily Dickinson speaks most universally precisely because she speaks so concretely. In speaking of a thing with feathers, she bypasses some of the debates that too often divide religious people as they name, and sometimes cling to, their ultimates: the Lord, the Abyss, the Universe, the All, the Mystery. However, if we imagine hope as a bird, we need to remember that, unlike a tangible bird, hope cannot be located in a particular region of space to the exclusion of other regions, and it cannot be grasped with the hands or seen with the eye. Its song is universal yet perpetually adapted to each new situation. Consequently, my suggestion is that today we experience the song of the thing with feathers through five challenges, five callings, five melodies. Taken together, they form a single song that is both a collective challenge and a collective hope.

WHEN RELIGION MEETS SCIENCE

To these five challenges, all of which concern life and death, we can add still another which can sometimes seem slightly less urgent and a bit more academic but which, in the long run, may be equally important. It is the challenge to engage in meaningful dialogue with the natural sciences, trustful that science and religion together add more wisdom to the human experience than do either considered alone. For religious people, the challenge is to learn from science while at the same time avoiding the lure of scientism. Scientism is the view that scientific ways of knowing are the only legitimate ways of knowing and that religious ways of knowing—through prayer and meditation, intuition and imagination, worship and love—are deluded. The challenge for religious people is to welcome science while avoiding this kind of epistemological reductionism. It is to know that we learn something about nature from scientific experimentation and that we also learn something about nature from taking walks in the woods and listening to the prayers of birds.

With a balanced approach to science, one understands that science does indeed have much to offer religion. For example, with its emphasis on evolutionary change over time and its methods of experimentation, science can help those of us who are religious to live more flexibly and self-critically. It can show us that letting go of maladaptive habits of thought and feeling, even if they were effective adaptations at an earlier time, is part of the way life naturally unfolds and that creatively adapting to new situations leads to evolutionary success. We can come to see our own most fervent convictions not as absolutes that fall from the sky but rather as experiments with truth, experiments that can be subject to change and correction.

Moreover, with its emphasis on the earth as a small planet nested within the larger context of an evolving galactic process, science can help religious people de-center themselves and adopt an ecological outlook on life. It can remind us not only that we are kin to other creatures on the planet, both biologically and spiritually, but also that we are small yet included participants in a larger galactic whole that is amazing and vast. This sense of being small yet included can soften our tendencies to think that we are the center of the universe, and it can lighten the load of thinking that our suffering, and ours alone, is what matters in the cosmic scheme of things. More positively, it can help restore a sense of divine transcendence, not by appealing to a separate being who resides three miles off the planet, but by pointing to a greater grandeur within which we live and move and have our being: the universe itself. To the monotheists of the world—Muslims and Jews and Christians, for example—the grandeur can rightly be seen as a natural sacrament, a visible sign of an invisible grace. Islam teaches that all natural forms are *ayat*, signs of this Transcendence, and thus that each star, in its own way, is an *ayatollah*. Science can help enliven our awareness of the signs.

It is in the larger context of these various challenges that I write this book. My focus is on the fifth challenge—welcoming religious diversity—while keeping in mind the others. Although I write as a Christian, I do not write for Christians alone but for people of all religions who are interested in religious diversity and also for people who are spiritually interested but not religiously affiliated. To explain for whom I write, a story is in order.

ON BEING SPIRITUAL BUT NOT RELIGIOUS

I am a college teacher of world religions and often on the first day of class I will give students an index card and ask them to tell me something about themselves. Without defining the terms in advance, I ask them to let me know whether they think of themselves as spiritual, or religious, or both. Typically they respond in one of four ways.

"I am *spiritual but not religious*."

"I am *both spiritual and religious*."

"I am *neither spiritual nor religious*, and I'm not sure why I'm taking this class in the first place."

"I am *religious but not spiritual* because I really don't know what you mean by spirituality."

Those who say "I am spiritual but not religious" are among my most sensitive students. In speaking of themselves as "spiritual," they are not boasting. They are not suggesting that they are deeper or better or wiser than other people but simply that they are interested in spiritual matters not only academically but personally. They mean that they have feelings of spiritual awareness at various points in their lives, that they have a depth dimension to their lives, and that they think there is something more to the universe than the random shuffling of atoms and molecules. In saying that they are "not religious," they mean that they are not affiliated with a particular religious tradition. This means that they do not participate in rituals and other institutionalized forms of religious practice and that they do not claim a particular religious tradition as their own. Their reasons for not affiliating are manifold. Sometimes it is because they sense that the world's religions try to contain or possess the spiritual dimension of life, and they believe that it cannot be so easily contained. Sometimes it is because they have been burned by an overly authoritarian form of religious life and do not want that to happen again. Sometimes it is because they have become convinced that religions are ultimately forces of prejudice and arrogance and violence, and that they must be rejected rather than accepted. And sometimes it is simply because they do not find the various claims of the world religions plausible, perhaps in light of the findings of modern science. Often they will say that their church is the natural world because their deepest sense of spirituality emerges in communion with the rest of creation, during walks in the woods or time spent by the ocean. This leads them to say: "I am not Christian or Buddhist or Muslim, but there is a spiritual side to my life that is important to me. All things considered, I may be spiritual, but I am not religious."

By contrast, those who say "I am spiritual and religious" find that one or another of the world's religions can be a hospitable context for spiritual pilgrimage. They know that the religions can be sources of evil in the world, but they also know that something deep and rich can be gained by participating in the rituals, by being connected to a community, and by listening to the challenges and claims that come from the religions themselves. They fear that, without such participation on their part, an allegedly spiritual pilgrimage might too easily become a consumer-driven smorgasbord approach to spiritual truth, in which a person simply picks and chooses among various spiritual options without tasting the depth of any of them. They realize that when this happens, it is the ego, not the reality of spiritual truth, that too often serves as the guide to life. This leads them to believe that, at least for them, one or another of the world's religions—Christianity or Islam or Judaism or Buddhism—is an important and perhaps necessary context for authentic spiritual seeking. As one Christian put it to me, "I find God in community with fellow seekers in my church, in our singing together, praying together, and serving the poor together. Without them, I trust God would still be with me, but I'm not sure that I would be with God. The community helps keep me honest."

Then there are those who say "I am neither spiritual nor religious." They usually mean something like, "I think I know what religion is, and I don't want to have much to do with it; I am suspicious of the word 'spirituality' because it is too often used as a way of allowing religion—especially belief in God—to creep into discussions." Some are reacting to an overly authoritarian form of religious upbringing in which God has been envisioned like a policeman in the sky who forever keeps a person in guilt and forbids honest questioning. They suspect that spirituality is just a way of bringing God-the-policeman back into the picture, albeit by another name. And, like some who are "spiritual but not religious," they are troubled by the evil that religion has caused in human life, often in the very name of God. Somehow, in the process of reacting to these things, they have decided that there is not "something more" to the universe besides the material world. Accordingly, they are trying to live, and perhaps succeeding in living, in a strictly secular way, looking to find life's meaning exclusively in friendships, creative activity, respect for life, and, in some cases, the pleasures of consumer society. They see religion and spirituality as human constructs developed out of a human search for meaning, and they seek to live more honestly without the illusions of such constructs.

The final group consists of those who say "I am religious but not spiritual." Often they are Christian and they are active in churches, either in a perfunctory way or in a more engaged way. But they are not sure that there exists something called "spirituality" that can be separated from participation in such communities. For them, the only genuine meaning for the word "spirituality" lies in fidelity to the teachings of a religious tradition and enactment of its practices. Spirituality is singing the hymns and reading the Bible, praying before meals and helping the poor. It is not something deeper or more inward or something mystical. It is organized religion itself as lived from the inside in community with others. In my own experience, some of the best people I know fall into this category. They are un-pretentious, un-self-preoccupied, and humble.

Of course, these four groups lie on a spectrum, and some among my students—like some in the world—shift from one position to another in the course of a day or even an hour. I know that I myself have days when I am "spiritual but not religious" and days when I am "neither spiritual nor religious," even as I have days when I feel "both religious and spiritual." For my part, I think that the Christian life involves a sense of grace and a freedom to be all of these things.

My point, however, is that I am writing this book on world religions with all four approaches in mind and I find myself sometimes trying to speak to one group and sometimes to another. I hope that you, my reader, can identify with at least one of these groups some of the time. Indeed, I am especially hopeful that some of my readers are "spiritual but not religious" or "neither spiritual nor religious" because, in my view, they—you—have a special role in the future of religion. People who are "spiritual but not religious" and "neither spiritual nor religious" serve as prophetic reminders that, without self-criticism, religion is blind indeed.

Nevertheless, because much of this book is explicitly addressed to people who think of themselves as both spiritual and religious, I want to say a special word to them—to us. It is we who have a special stake in the religious institutions of the world, whether Muslim or Jewish or Christian or Buddhist or otherwise, and it is we who have a special responsibility to help our traditions address the five challenges named earlier, including the challenge to welcome diversity.

There are at least two ways to welcome diversity. One is to personally get to know people of other religions, spending time with them and working together to help build local communities that are just, sustainable, and peaceful. In many parts of the world there are ecumenical organizations aimed toward this end, and these organizations are a sign of great hope. The second way to welcome diversity is to undertake critical, yet friendly, readings of the other religions—even if we do not know people who belong to them—with an interest in appreciating the wisdom those religions might offer us. Both of these ways are very important. They are acts of peacemaking, because they help create a culture of peace—of open-mindedness and open-heartedness—in the community where we live and, more generally, in the larger world. To get to know people of other religions and to undertake friendly readings of their traditions is akin to lighting a candle that helps brighten our small corner of the world, helping to dispel the blindness that permeates the region. When this small candle is combined with other candles in other parts of the world, it can provide hope for a world too often torn apart by fear, hatred, and confusion. There is a great need in our world for this kind of candle lighting.

Among religious people, of course, a primary obstacle to such candle lighting is fear. Some of this fear is justified. The world's religions contain tendencies within themselves toward arrogance and violence against which we must guard our hearts and sometimes our lives. But religions are like human beings; they can be simultaneously good in some ways and evil in other ways. Consequently, part of the fear is unjustified. We fear what is unfamiliar and new to us in other religions just because it is new and unfamiliar, and we also fear that, if we open ourselves to other religions, we will lose what is most important about our own. We fall into the trap of thinking that, if we are rooted in the best of our own tradition, we cannot be open to the richness of others. If we have roots—so we believe—we cannot also have wings.

What many people seek today is a way of being religious that involves strong roots and healthy wings, neither to the exclusion of the other. They want to be rooted in the best of their religious traditions and in the deeper revelations of the universe, and they want to be open to new ideas that come from other religions, from science, and from fresh revelations of the spirit. It is this kind of religion that can enable people to live lightly on the earth and gently with each other. It is this kind of religion that can help people make peace between religions. And it is this kind of religion that I will be promoting in this book. In what follows I explain my approach.

WHITEHEAD AND THE WORLD RELIGIONS

As noted above, five days a week for nine months of the year, I teach world religions to college undergraduates. In my courses, my aim is to teach the religions critically but also empathetically, helping my students understand what it might be like to be inside the skin of a Hindu or a Buddhist, a Muslim or a Jew, looking out at the world from his or her own perspective, and inspired by the ideals of the religion at issue.

Over the years, I have discovered a common pattern among some of my more conservative students. Many of them arrive in class with their guard up, having determined in advance that if one religion—namely their own—is true, then the others must be false. To be more precise, they arrive believing that if their religion contains the most important kind of truth—truth relevant to salvation—then the other religions cannot have any of this truth even though they might contain other less important truths.

Several years ago, I was reflecting on the beliefs of the more conservative students when the grandson of Mahatma Gandhi, Arun, visited my campus. We were having lunch together, and I explained the situation to him. He listened to me, was silent for a while, and then quietly asked if these students were Jewish or Christian or Muslim. I said most of them were Christian, and he offered an interesting observation. He explained that, at least in his own experience, members of the Abrahamic family of religions sometimes equate religion with the possession of already-revealed divine truth, whereas his grandfather equated religion with the pursuit of truth not yet attained.

In saying this, he put his finger on something that I myself bring to the college classroom. As I teach the world religions to college undergraduates, I bring the hope, characteristic of most college professors trained in the West, that my students will be engaged in a pursuit of truth and that they will bracket, to some degree, their pre-determined commitments to truths already revealed to them. Indeed, I bring this hope not only as a liberal arts teacher but as a friend to the Abrahamic religions. The Abrahamic religions emphasize openness to God. Some lineages within these religions propose that God and Truth are two names for the same reality, such that openness to God involves openness to Truth as guided by experience, reason, tradition, and scripture. For most Jews and Christians and Muslims, the heart of this openness lies in a recognition that all humans are in the situation of Abraham who, as the Bible says, was called by God into an unknown future and who had to let go of familiar securities in order to respond to that call. For religious people today, the "familiar securities" are not necessarily the physical comforts that Abraham enjoyed in Ur but rather those psychological comforts, sometimes taken as absolute certainties, that block people from openness to other religions and from future revelation. One of the deepest and most pernicious of these securities is that internal habit of mind which says, "I already have all the truth and there is nothing left to learn." This internal habit is a false god in its own right because it prevents a person from recognizing what

Muslims mean when they say *"Allahu Akbar"* or "God is Great." They do not simply mean that God is bigger and more powerful than all other beings. They mean that God is a deep and all-pervading mystery, everywhere at once, incomparable to any finite thing we know and yet closer to us than our jugular veins.

About four weeks into the course, things often change for the students, despite their initial resistance. My students become more Gandhian, more open to continuing revelation. They have been influenced by Huston Smith, whose classic text, *The World's Religions*, inspires them to be moved by the various kinds of wisdom found in each religion, despite initial inclinations to the contrary.[3] As Smith readily admits, his book is weak on history and social context, and it does not dwell on the darker and more oppressive sides of religious life which I will discuss later in this book. This is why many teachers of world religions supplement his text with other introductory texts.

Still, at least in my own experience, Smith's book is unparalleled in its capacity to inspire students to take the wisdom of the world's religions seriously. He moves from religion to religion, imagining himself inside the skin of people who are drawn to the religion from the inside, and making the case for that religion as its practitioners might make the case. The results are transforming. Smith inspires my students not only to learn about the religions but also to learn from them, even after they have completed the class.

As this conversion occurs, I often see an idea emerging in their minds. It is a threefold idea, namely that (1) each religion has its own distinctive wisdom, resulting from trial and error over many generations of spiritual seeking, (2) no single religion has all the wisdom relevant to human flourishing, and (3) there is more inherited wisdom in all the world religions added together than in any of them considered alone. Smith gives my students a phrase to name this threefold possibility. He speaks of the world's religions at their best as the *distilled wisdom* of the human race. Many of my students add a fourth component.

They begin to suspect that, even if someone were to pull together all this distilled wisdom, there would still be more wisdom to discover than any of the religions have yet discovered.

Some of these students are science majors. They arrive in class believing that science itself is a wisdom tradition, albeit a new one that has emerged somewhat recently in world history, compared to the more traditional religions. As I ask these students what they appreciate about science, I often get two responses. They appreciate the insights concerning nature that science offers, such as the idea that the universe is evolving over time and that there is indeterminacy within the very depths of matter. And they appreciate what they like to call "the scientific method."

As one who spends a great deal of time treating religions that appeal to divine revelation, I find their appreciation of the scientific method quite understandable. They like the fact that the scientific method, whatever it is, relies for wisdom not on divine revelation or private mystical insights but rather on observation, theorizing, and replicable experiments that can confirm or falsify a theory. For them, there is something fresh and promising in this way of seeking knowledge, particularly when compared to the worst aspects of appealing to revelation as found in some religions. If they believe the unfolding of human history has involved continuing revelation, then they see science itself as part of that revelation.

This takes me to what happens in about the fifth week of class. A question naturally emerges in the minds of all of the students: *Has anyone tried to synthesize the best wisdom from religion and science in such a way that it is plausible to the scientific mind and yet meaningful to the advocates of the religions?* It is at this stage that I often wish my students were simultaneously taking a course in the philosophy of Whitehead, precisely because it can help a person appreciate and interpret the wisdom of the world's religions in a way that enriches, rather than contradicts, the methods and insights of the natural sciences.

Whitehead offers what we might call an *acoustic vision of reality,* not in the sense that he thinks that everything that happens in the world is beautiful in the way music can be beautiful, but in the sense that our experience of the world around us is, in its own way, a form of deep listening, in which "the listener" and the "listened to" cannot be sharply separated. The universe is not simply a visual universe; it is even more deeply a sound-sensitive universe, a sonoral universe in which the very reality of sound offers a metaphor for understanding the deeper nature of things.

By sound, in this context, I do not mean sound as understood in the natural sciences. I do not mean the striking of sound waves against the ear drum, but rather the experience of hearing sound from a first-person perspective, however this hearing might be further analyzed in terms of physics and chemistry. Consider listening to music in a live concert. If we close our eyes while listening, we realize that the sound of the music is inside us and outside us at the same time, such that we would have a difficult time saying exactly where it is. It is present in us, and yet it is also beyond us. It is this sensation—this feeling of something being both part of us and more than us—that is at the heart of an acoustic vision of reality. I would suggest that this experience of something being within us and beyond us is revelatory of the very nature of reality.

I borrow the phrase "an acoustic vision of reality" from the composer and philosopher David Dunn, who uses these words to explore the possibility that the world is best understood through an analogy to sound rather than one to sight.[4] Dunn addresses the issue in explaining connections between music and wilderness experience.

> I wonder if music might be a way of mapping reality through metaphors of sound, paralleling the visually dominant metaphors of speech and written symbols. I think that most musicians can relate to the idea that music is not just something we do to amuse ourselves. It is a *different way of thinking about the world,* a way to remind ourselves of a prior wholeness when the mind of the forest was not something out there, separate in the world, but something of which we were an intrinsic part.[5]

In the spirit of Dunn, then, what Whitehead offers is a different and more musical way of thinking about the world that is sensitive to the "prior wholeness" from which all human experience emerges, moment by moment. Like Dunn, he is critical of ways of thinking about reality that rely exclusively on visual metaphors. Whitehead's aim in his book *Process and Reality* is to illuminate the earlier and more fundamental aspects of an occasion of experience, aspects that do not have the sense of separation so characteristic of visual experience and that Dunn suggests may be better revealed through music than through many other media.

A sense of this prior wholeness, which for Whitehead is the deeper background of each and every moment of our lives, does not eliminate a sense of individuality or a capacity to act in the world in a creative way. However, such a sense can help a person to act in ways that are cooperative, rather than competitive, with the healing impulses in life. This is why an acoustic vision of reality can be so important in an age needful of peace. It can help people let go of impulses toward self-centered satisfaction and contribute more effectively to a wider world of which they are already a part.

Imagine, for example, two items of visual perception: two small boxes on a table. They have sharp edges that enable us to separate them from their background, and they seem completely separate from each other. The two boxes seem self-contained as well; if you move one of them, the other is not changed. Now compare the visual image of these boxes to, say, the sounds of music in a live concert. Like boxes, the sounds have distinctive identities: a C-sharp is not a B-flat. But the sounds are wave-like rather than particulate, which means that they are not simply located in one region of space and not present in others. They do not have sharp edges. Moreover, their identities emerge in relationship to, not apart from, other sounds in the performance. A B-flat in relation to a C-sharp is different from a B-flat in relation to an E-flat. Equally important, when we hear these sounds, they are inside us as well as outside us, and we are partly composed of the sounds being heard. This means that we ourselves, as experiencing subjects, do not have sharp edges either. We are not encapsulated egos cut off from the world by the boundaries of our skin but beings-in-the-world who are partly composed of the world we are in. Things can be outside our bodies but, nevertheless, inside our experience.

This is how Whitehead looks at the world. In *Process and Reality*, he writes that the primary purpose of his philosophy is to elicit recognition of the inter-being or inter-existence of all things:

> In fact if we allow for degrees of relevance, and for negligible relevance, we must say that every actual entity is present in every other actual entity. The philosophy of organism is mainly devoted to the task of making clear the notion of "being present in another entity." (PR 50)

[handwritten margin note: Whitehead → interconnection]

In a Whiteheadian context, therefore, peace is not simply cooperating creatively with others; it is also a form of inter-being, of communion, in which the participants have awakened to the fact that they share in one another's destinies because all destinies are interconnected.

Consequently, the contemporary challenge for world religions is to have participants undertake a journey toward this kind of peace, cognizant that peace can never be fully realized in life but that even small tastes of it are well worth the effort. Many among these participants—Jews, Christians, Muslims, Buddhists, Hindus, Sikhs, and a host of others—will simultaneously hope that even small experiences of peace, of beauty-in-the-making, in this life are part of what one Whiteheadian philosopher—David Ray Griffin—calls the continuing journey toward "peaceable selves" after death.[6] As Griffin makes clear, this hope for continuation after death is consistent with the deepest convictions of natural science, which, as interpreted through a Whiteheadian philosophy of science, likewise point to differences between the mind and the brain, such that the mind might continue after death. Such a hope is consistent with earthly hopes for peace on earth. Indeed, hope for life after death can energize our earthly aspirations. As Griffin puts it:

> The belief that we are on a spiritual journey, a journey in which there will be sufficient time to travel to reach our destination, can motivate us to think creatively about things we can do now, socially and even internationally as well as individually, to help ourselves move closer here and now to what we should be.

In a process context, contemporary efforts toward peace between religions are part of a larger journey toward a beauty that includes awareness of our interconnectedness. Even as we may be separated in time and space, we are knit together in a seamless web of connections. As the gifted Zen poet and teacher Thich Nhat Hanh puts it, we are because we inter-are.[7]

Let me summarize. Whitehead pictures the whole of the universe in a dynamic and relational way. He thinks of the universe as a community of subjects rather than a collection of objects, a web of creative and interdependent events embraced by a divine reality—a Deep Listening—who not only shares in the feelings of all living beings but also is present within all living beings as an indwelling lure toward satisfying existence. For Whitehead, God is not the supreme exception to inter-being but rather the supreme exemplification of it. God is in all things, and all things are in God, such that neither can be sharply separated from the other. Of course, this indwelling lure—God—is not within humans alone. It is also within plants and animals, hills and rivers, planets and stars. In Whitehead's philosophy, God is not merely anthropocentric; God is eco-centric and and each living being has its own unique relationship to the cosmic lure. Dogs respond to the lure of God by barking, cats by purring, fish by swimming, and birds by flying. But we human beings are likewise creatures among creatures, which means that we also experience the divine lure in a unique way, namely as an indwelling lure toward wisdom and compassion and healthy creativity in relation to the situation at hand. Whitehead believed that the many world religions, along with science and art and philosophy, can be responsive to this indwelling lure, each in its own way. Wherever we see wisdom and compassion and healthy creativity, we see God being God.

CHRISTIANITY AND THE CALL TO LISTEN

So far I have explained that, as a teacher of world religions, I have often wished that my students were familiar with Whitehead's philosophy. As I mentioned earlier, this book emerged from two of the roles I play in life. In addition to being a college teacher, I am also a believing Christian who has been actively involved in dialogues with Buddhists and Muslims for many years. When I speak from a Christian point of view, I bring with me a Whiteheadian, or process, understanding of Christianity. This means that I envision Christianity not so much as a prescribed path that must be traveled to reach an already-defined destination but more as a way of walking that can accommodate many different paths. It does not require repeating the beliefs of Jesus or imitating his every action. But it does involve a desire to walk in Christ's footsteps, day by day and moment by moment. The aim of Christians is to be open to God in our way and our time, as Jesus was in his way and his time. In the words of John Cobb, "We cannot go back to Jesus if that would mean simply repeating his belief. We can only go forward in a way that somehow corresponds in our time to the meaning of his life and message for the men of his time."[8]

With its emphasis on openness, a Whiteheadian approach to Christianity is continuous with Christian traditions that emphasize *humility* and *listening to others* and *welcoming the stranger* as defining characteristics of an authentic Christian spirituality. Christian traditions that emphasize these three traits are in tension with more aggressive Christian orientations that emphasize proclaiming the gospel in word and deed even before listening to others and finding out about their experience. These more aggressive Christian orientations also emphasize protecting oneself from others, including strangers, who might sully Christian purity. Some Christians have gravitated toward a theology of openness while others have gravitated toward a theology of self-protection; some toward a theology of listening and others toward a theology of proclamation.

In Western Christianity, one of the most inspiring examples of a theology of listening can be found in the monastic tradition of the St. Benedict. Benedictine ways of thinking can well be appropriated, and are appropriated, in non-monastic settings. In many respects the Benedictine approach to Christian life resembles a Whiteheadian approach. The Benedictines envision the Christian life as a combination of work and prayer in ordinary life, neither to the exclusion of the other, and they emphasize that this combination is best accomplished in community with others, with a deep impulse toward hospitality to strangers. Similarly, Whiteheadian Christians emphasize these things, adding that "community" includes plants and animals, hills and rivers, trees and stars. This enriched understanding of community is quite consistent with Benedictine thinking, which itself involves a commitment to be faithful to places and not just to people.

Interestingly, the similarity between Whiteheadian Christianity and Benedictine Christianity runs still deeper with what the Benedictines call a *spirituality of awareness* as distinct from a *spirituality of consolation*. A spirituality of consolation identifies spiritual well-being with consoling and peaceful states of consciousness, such that everyday emotional states—boredom and sadness and sleepiness—are thought to be less spiritual than heightened states of consciousness. On the other hand, a *spirituality of awareness* is more Buddhist in tone, identifying spiritual well-being with cognizance of what is happening in each present moment, no matter what is happening. Benedictine spirituality is oriented toward a spirituality of awareness. At the very heart of it is deep listening to others, human and non-human alike, with sensitivity to experience.[9]

What is this listening? For Benedictines, listening is a metaphor for empathic presence to others with an interest in affirming and honoring their well-being. It is noteworthy that this way of feeling is called "listening" rather than "seeing," because, as most of us know through the experience of listening to music, listening has a quality that is not always present in seeing. In seeing things, we often have a sense that there is a dichotomy, a separation, between subject and object. In looking at a table, for example, we may feel the table is out there, two or three feet in front of our eyes, whereas we are in here, two inches behind our eyeballs. Not all visual perception has this quality, but much of it does.

On the other hand, as noted earlier, in listening to music that we enjoy, the dichotomy between "outside" and "inside" is not as sharp because the sounds that we hear out there in the room do not have sharp edges in our phenomenal field, and they are also within our minds. It is very difficult, if not impossible, to separate our listening to the music from the music itself. This does not mean that, even as we listen to the music, we cannot also separate ourselves from it, analyzing it as we listen. But the "object" from which we separate ourselves, namely the music, is within us, not outside us. There is a sense in which, for good or ill, we are the music being listened to, even as we can reflect on the music and thus transcend it.

Joan Chittister points out that Benedictines understand the Christian vocation as a call to listen to others with an interest in affirming and honoring their well-being. The things that we hear, namely the feelings of others and the others who feel them, are part of who and what we are, even as they are more than us. Such listening has a wisdom to it because, in feeling the feelings of others, we understand who they are, what their aims are, what they are seeking, what is important to them. In this sense, the listening is also a seeing—if by "seeing" we mean being illumined or becoming aware of something that we had not previously known. But it is an intuitive and empathic illumination, not a clear and distinct illumination, because it is dealing with feelings, and feelings do not have clear edges. Equally important, the listening may be wrong. We may think we are hearing what others say and thus feeling their feelings, only to realize that we were not hearing them at all because we were projecting too much onto them from our own experience. Thus, listening involves and requires a commitment to keep listening and to be willing, amid this listening, to be corrected again and again. The Benedictine claim is that this listening and this commitment to it are part of the very substance of Christian spirituality, especially as it accents a spirituality of awareness. The listening need not occur only with the ears but can also occur with the help of the eyes and with touch and with a host of other capacities, including the imagination. The unique feature of listening is that it is empathic. It is, in the words of Saint Benedict, "listening with the ear of the heart."[10]

This way of thinking deeply resonates with Whiteheadian thinking. Like the Benedictines, Whitehead affirms that empathic feeling—pre-linguistic empathy with the feelings of others—is the ground of all immediate experience, and he asserts that active and reflective responses to what is felt come after, not before, the empathy. Whitehead's *Process and Reality* proposes that, in the beginning of each moment of human experience and in the beginning of each moment of divine consciousness, there is a taking into account—a "prehending"—of something that is given for experience (PR 42–45). In human consciousness, this "something that is given for experience" may be a person or an animal, an energy in the body or a dimly discerned fantasy in the imagination, a memory from the past or a hope for the future; or it may simply be the internal chattering of the mind. Ultimately, says Whitehead, the something that is given for experience is the universe itself as expressed in, but also more than, the particular object that is given for experience. Whitehead coins the term "concrescence" to name the way in which the many things of the universe "become one" in the immediacy of the moment (PR 21–22).

If we look at the process of concrescence from a third-person perspective, as if it were something we were diagramming on a blackboard, we might position the already-determined universe just to the left of the process of experiencing. We might draw it like this:

The snowflakes on the left represent the already-decided events of the past; the clouds on the right represent not-yet-decided events in the future; the point of intersection represents the vantage point of the experiencing subject as that subject pre-hends (takes into account) the already-decided past and not-yet-decided future; and the flames represent the various ways in which the prehending subject can integrate the past and future (as potentiality) into a meaningful whole in the present. The many events in the past are the items that "become one" in the process of concrescence such that the process of concrescence is itself a "concrescence of the universe" (PR 51). The letter "I" in the center of the middle flame represents the ideal possibility for integrating the myriad influences inherited from the past: that is, the particular possibility available in experience which, if actualized by the experiencer, embodies maximum harmony and intensity relative to the circumstances at hand. It may be a possibility for forgiveness, or creativity, or honest questioning, or laughter; in any case it is, if actualized, the grace sufficient to the moment. In process thought this ideal is understood to be from God, even as it emerges out of the immediate situation; and the experiencing subject feels this possibility with an inner eros to realize it and thus participate in the Eros of God. By Eros, I mean the tendency, the aim, the desire deep within the cosmos for richness of experience, enjoyed by living beings, both human and non-human. Indeed, the hoped-for and energetically charged ideal is one way in which God is present in each and every moment of experience. This is the way the process of concrescence is often depicted in introductions to Whitehead's philosophy.

However, if we turn away from the diagram altogether and imagine ourselves inside the process of the many-becoming-one, we realize that the universe—the many that are becoming one—is not "back there" to the left but rather "right here" where we are sitting or standing or lying down. The universe is in the present. If we are talking to another person, the universe is present as this person right in front of us with whom we are talking; if we are eating a meal, the universe is the very food on our plate, the food that we are eating; if we are mourning the death of a loved one, the universe is this loved one who is now absent from us and whom we miss deeply. To be sure, these realities do not exhaust the whole of the universe, and it is good to think about other things, too. We cannot always focus on the food on our table or on the people we are talking to. But they are incarnations of the whole of the universe as present within our experience, and we meet the universe through them. Each face, each blade of grass, each frog, each dream is given for experience—and our task is to receive and creatively respond to what is given. As Buddhists emphasize, we are always and inevitably in the present moment of experiencing something, and this moment begins with an act of reception, of feeling something, of welcoming a stranger. In the beginning is the listening.

As a moment of experience occurs, this listening is filled with aliveness. It is part of what Whitehead calls the "subjective immediacy" of experience itself.[11] But in the course of a human life, this immediacy is perishing from one moment to the next, such that a person can never hold onto it. We can enjoy the immediacy or suffer the immediacy or sleep through the immediacy, but we can never cling to it because it changes from moment to moment as we do. Whiteheadian thinkers are often called "process" thinkers, and the word "process" is meant both to name the process of experiencing as it begins with listening and to suggest that reality itself is first and foremost a process of flux and flow, changing at every instant and new at every moment, such that there is much to love and appreciate but nothing so solid that it can be held onto forever. This idea is very Buddhist insofar as Buddhists emphasize not clinging to a world in flux, and it is no accident that Whiteheadians and Buddhists have much in common, since both recognize what Whitehead calls the "perpetual perishing" of subjective immediacy.[12] This idea is very Christian and Jewish and Muslim, because these traditions also recognize that the word "forever" is rightly applied only to God. Process thinkers add that even the "forever-ness" of God is in process, which means that even God cannot be clung to as a solid object among solid objects. Of course, many Jews and Christians and Muslims agree. Faith in God, they say, is not clinging to God as if God were an object among objects but rather trusting in God as a subject among subjects who is everywhere at once, feeling the emotions of the world and responding with "tender care that nothing be lost."[13] When they pray, they think of God as hearing the prayer not *before* they pray but rather *as* they pray.

This image of a universe in process, and even a God in process, has deep implications for Christians who feel called to listen. It means that our process of listening never ceases because there is always more to be heard, to be felt, to be listened to, than has yet been heard. The spiritual life is an ongoing and lifelong process of conversion in which our hearts are continually transformed by what we hear. As Chittister writes,

> Benedictine spirituality is the spirituality of an open heart. A willingness to be touched. A sense of otherness. There is no room for isolated splendor or self-sufficiency. Here all of life becomes a teacher and we its students. The listener can always learn and turn and begin again. The open can always be filled. The real discipline can always be surprised by God.[14]

In an age that is increasingly aware of religious pluralism and religious people's need to listen to one another, Whitehead's philosophy can help all Christians and many others become better listeners and more Benedictine in spirit. It can help facilitate a capacity for deep listening in which the subjective aims and feelings of people of other religions are heard and understood even when those aims are at odds with those of the listener. It can also facilitate a listening in which their wisdom, expressed in words but also in sighs too deep for words, is appreciated and learned from in a process of ongoing conversion. For the Christian, this way of approaching other religions can unfold with a trust that wherever there is wisdom of any sort, whether in religion or science or secular humanism, this wisdom is of and from the very God revealed in Jesus even though it may not be about the God revealed in Jesus. As Chittister says, we can be "surprised by God," and often this surprise will come through the minds and hearts and faces of people of other traditions in whom God is present. This does not mean that other religions, or our own for that matter, are completely filled with divine sweetness and light. There is a sad and tragic side to religion as well. A good bit of it. I will be addressing this in chapter 2. But for now, I want to place what has just been said in the larger context of the five challenges faced by the world's religions.

THE WHOLE WORLD IS A MONASTERY

From a Whiteheadian or process perspective, the five challenges faced by the world religions can be approached at three different levels: intellectual understanding, practical action, and spiritual awareness. An intellectual response to the challenges will seek to affirm beliefs that are plausible, given what we know of the world through direct experience, and that are consonant with the contemporary need to live with respect and care for the community of life. A practical response will be actively engaged in the building of communities that are socially just, ecologically sustainable, and spiritually satisfying. And a

[handwritten margin note: Levels of response]

spiritual response will involve the cultivation of spiritual states of awareness—such as listening and amazement, delight in beauty, and a trust in something more than the human ego—that are conducive to such respect and care. These three levels of response correspond to three dimensions of religious life that are found in many of the world religions. Buddhists speak of them as understanding, moral conduct, and meditation; Muslims often speak of them as practicing the five pillars *(islam)*, understanding the teachings *(iman)*, and doing the beautiful *(ihsan)*; Christians might speak of them as theological understanding, love-in-action, and prayer. Of course, the three-fold division, as embodied in these three traditions, has different nuances and tonalities. Meditation is not the same as prayer, and practicing the five pillars is not reducible to love-in-action. Still, many traditions speak of three dimensions of healthy religious life, and the divisions have a certain commonality. Emphasizing this commonality, we can speak of the three dimensions mentioned above: intellectual understanding, practical action, and spiritual awareness.

In introducing Benedictine spirituality, I focused on the third dimension. I proposed that Whitehead's philosophy recognizes that spiritual awareness includes, above all, a willingness to listen to others on their own terms and for their own sakes. However, this philosophy is also conducive to the other two levels and, before concluding this chapter, I want to focus on a more theological level, showing where a process approach fits into the larger scheme of contemporary Christian theologies of dialogue. I suspect that many of the world's monotheistic religions can learn from two of the approaches that have developed within contemporary Christianity: the mutuality and acceptance approaches.

In *Introducing Theologies of Religions*, Paul Knitter shows how in recent Christian history four attitudes toward other world religions have emerged: a "replacement" model, a "fulfillment" model, a "mutuality" model, and an "acceptance" model. The replacement model says that Christianity possesses the only truth relevant to salvation and that it ought to replace all the other religions. The fulfillment model acknowledges that there can be saving wisdom in other world religions, but that this wisdom is completed or made whole by Christian revelation. The mutuality model says that Christians can enter into dialogue with people of other religions in a spirit of mutual enquiry, learning, and sharing with others, trustful that wherever there is truth it is of God and from God, thus named or not. The acceptance model says that Christians can accept the sheer plurality of religions, cognizant not only of different truths but also of different, and sometimes incompatible, forms of salvation.[15]

Process theology recommends what might best be called a mutuality approach. As noted above, it proposes that wherever there is wisdom of any sort, it is inwardly inspired by God. This means that people can enter into dialogue with one another, trustful that they are inwardly inspired by a common lure toward wisdom, but it does not mean that the parties in dialogue are all "saying the same thing." What a Buddhist knows in awakening to the irreducibility of impermanence—or the sheer suchness of things as they are—may be different from what a Christian knows in awakening to God's love, although from a Whiteheadian perspective there is wisdom in both forms of knowing, since impermanence is an essential dimension of the nature of things, and since, as I explain in chapter 3, there truly is a God who loves the world amid its impermanence. Here love, whether divine or human, means sharing in the joys and sufferings of living beings and acting in ways that seek their well-being. In Whitehead's philosophy, God is both empathic in this way and active in this way, albeit through invitation rather than coercion. This invitation is what is meant by the divine lure, and it is a lure toward wisdom, which includes, among other things, wisdom concerning impermanence. The point here, then, is that both forms of wisdom—wisdom concerning impermanence and wisdom concerning God—may be inspired by the indwelling lure toward wisdom. Precisely because Buddhists and Christians have awakened to different truths, they can talk with one another and learn from each other in a spirit of mutual spiritual pilgrimage.

Ultimately, though, mutuality cannot be the whole story. There are times amid dialogue when religious people can and must disagree with one another. We must learn the arts of creative disagreement. These arts are needed today not only between religions but also within religions where sometimes dialogue is most difficult. In Christianity, for example, there are serious differences among Christians on many issues, ranging from the death penalty to homosexuality to the authority of scripture and the status of Jesus. Some Christians believe that Christianity is compatible with the death penalty, and others believe it is not. Some believe that God welcomes many different ways of being human, including those involving same-sex bonds; others believe that God requires only one way. Some believe that the Bible is culturally conditioned and fallible, and others believe it is inerrant. Some believe Jesus was God in human clothing; others believe that Jesus was a human called by God to reveal God's will. In short, Christians are diverse.

Here is where the acceptance model can be helpful. This model invites participants in dialogue to be honest about differences, to accept the fact that differences exist and that some of these differences are contradictory rather than complementary. Thus the word "acceptance" does not mean mutual agreement but *fidelity to the bonds of relationship even amid serious disagreement*. The acceptance model recognizes that argumentation can be part of the friendship, not only within religions but also between religions.

Is this asking too much of human beings? Are humans really capable of agreeing to disagree on matters that are extremely important to them? Most of us already have some taste of it in family life. In many families, individual family members have serious and vehement differences, but through fidelity to the bonds of relationship, the members of the family agree not to abandon one another but to keep talking. They are committed to continued relationship. As a lay associate in a Benedictine community, I know that the same applies to monastic communities. Such communities may have their moments of communal joy, but they are also ongoing experiments in communal living among people with different personalities and convictions. I mention the Benedictines because, in certain ways, the whole world has now become a single family trying to live in a single monastery without walls. In the words of Prophet Muhammad, "The whole earth is a mosque."[16] We are already within this monastery, this mosque, even if we do not like some of our companions. Our vocation is to hang in there together.

Interestingly, the fruits of agreeing to disagree can at times be quite beautiful. Sometimes the deepest and most powerful bonds humans can ever know have roots in acceptance of serious differences. Here, the Jewish tradition offers a special gift to the world, proposing that argumentation, even with God, can be a form of spirituality in its own right. If God can receive complaints and grievances and critiques without abandoning a deeper covenant with the world, then perhaps we humans can do the same in covenant with one another. Such is the best hope for the world. It is not that people will agree on all matters. It is that they will celebrate their commonalities, learn from complementary differences, and manage to live together amidst serious and irresolvable conflicts.

TWELVE PLANKS ON THE WHITEHEADIAN BRIDGE

In the previous two sections, I have emphasized the relevance of Whiteheadian or process theology to Christians who are seeking to be open to other religions. The larger claim of this book, however, is that this theology can also be relevant to people of other religions and, in a different way, to people who are spiritual but not religious. It is no accident that, even though most process theologians are Christian, some are also Buddhist, Jewish, Hindu, Bahai, and Muslim. Whitehead's philosophy offers an interpretive, but relatively neutral, conceptual vocabulary with which people of different religions can interpret their own wisdom while appreciating wisdom from others. In this way, it functions as a bridge between religions. It may be helpful to name some of the planks on this bridge.

Interdependence. The universe is a seamless web of interdependent events, and every event is dependent on, and present in, every other. In the world's religions, this idea is depicted deeply in those traditions that emphasize creation as a vast web of life and, perhaps most deeply, in Buddhism, which stresses the inter-existence or inter-being of all events.

Impermanence. The universe is constantly evolving, such that nothing stays the same for any two moments. In the world's religions, this idea is implicit in all traditions that speak of the world as a perpetual perishing of events and—again, perhaps most deeply—in Buddhism, which emphasizes the moment-by-moment character of all life.

Indeterminism. The energy of the universe is filled with creative spontaneity such that, even as events in the world are profoundly influenced by what has happened in the past, they are never entirely determined by their past. In modern science, this idea is presented most persuasively in quantum mechanics, which shows that, at a subatomic level, quantum events are momentary "happenings" that arise and then perish, succeeded by other happenings. In religious life, this same principle is exemplified in traditions that speak of a human capacity in each moment to respond creatively to inherited events and thus alter the course of the future. In Hinduism, this principle is found in the notion of karma, which sees in each experience in human life both an effect of previous causes and a cause of subsequent events.

Mind and Matter. Even ostensibly inorganic matter, at least at the quantum level, has mind-like properties, meaning that consciousness is an expression of, not an exception to, the kind of energy from which the universe as a whole emerges. There is an ontological continuity between physical energy and consciousness, a continuity of matter and mind. In religious life, this idea is found in traditions that see something like a life force in the whole of creation, a force expressed not only in human emotions but also in inorganic matter. Indigenous traditions seem especially sensitive to this continuity when they speak of the spirits of the earth and its many creatures.

Deep Listening. Amid cultural conditioning and unique historical contexts, humans have the capacity within themselves to listen to others on their own terms and for their own sakes without needing to reduce others to their own projections. Human capacities for deep listening are especially prized in the contemplative traditions of the many religions that emphasize being present to other people, to the surrounding world, and to God.

Value. All living beings are subjects of their own lives and not simply objects for others in that they have intrinsic value—that is, importance in and for themselves. A dog, for example, matters to itself and not simply to those around it, because it has awareness of its own and an interest in surviving with satisfaction. In this sense the dog has intrinsic value. Among the many world religions, Jainism seems especially sensitive to this notion of value, emphasizing that non-violence *(ahimsa)* applies not only to other human beings but also to all living beings that can suffer and feel pain.

God. There is a divine consciousness, everywhere at once, that includes all beings with a tender care that nothing be lost. Needless to say, this idea is found in the many monotheistic traditions of the world, including theistic forms of Hinduism (Shaivite and Vaishnavite), Pure Land Buddhism, and, of course, the Abrahamic traditions. Process theology emphasizes that God is both personal and transpersonal: a Thou to whom one can pray and in whose presence one can dance, and a spirit or energy that animates and guides each living being.

Creativity. The divine consciousness is an expression of, not an exception to, a continuous creativity—the Chinese call it *ch'i* and some Buddhists call it *sunyata*—of which all things are expressions. This spontaneity is the ultimate reality of the universe, a reality that Western mystical traditions sometimes call the Godhead. The divine consciousness—God—is the primordial, but not exclusive, instantiation of this creativity (more on this in chapter 3). A unique feature of process theology is that this creativity is non-teleological—or beyond good and evil—and thus expressed in all things, both good and evil. As embodied by each and every living being, it is the freedom—the capacity for self-creative decision—that each creature enjoys, moment by moment.

Persuasive Power. By virtue of this self-creativity, the power of God is necessarily limited, influential but not coercive. This means that in the universe things can happen that not even the divine reality can prevent. Process theologians point out the fact that divine power is persuasive rather than coercive when they wrestle with the problem of theodicy, or the explanation of God's goodness coexisting with evil; they suggest that divine power is not, and never has been, unilateral. This is consonant with numerous theological traditions, including biblical traditions, which emphasize that God is operative in the world as an indwelling call—a still small voice—rather than as a compelling power. It is this side of God that was emphasized by Gandhi when he spoke of divine truth as non-violent love.

Divine Empathy. Even as God is influential in the world as a continuous but not all-controlling power, the world is also influential in God. The experiences of living beings on earth and, more generally, the concrescences of all entities in the universe are experienced by God, not unlike the way in which experiences in a human body are experienced by the human being who has those experiences. What happens in the universe happens in God, such that God can be understood as an all-inclusive Empathy or Compassion who shares in the joys and sufferings of the world. Christians speak of this aspect of God as the Christic dimension of God; they say that it is that aspect of God which was revealed deeply, but not exclusively, in the passion of Christ on the cross. This aspect of God is also sensed in moments of personal prayer when, as a person prays, he or she intuitively senses that there is someone listening, like a sky-like mind that contains all that occurs. The empathic side of God is this Someone. It does not experience events on earth in advance of their occurrence, but rather on their occurrence, and is thus "in process" along with the world.

Many Forms of Salvation. The divine reality perpetually beckons each living being to live with satisfaction and, at least within the human sphere, to grow into the deepest form of wholeness—or peaceable selfhood—of which it is capable, and of which there are many kinds.

Life-after-Death. The journey toward peaceable selfhood, through one or another form of salvation, may continue after death until peaceable selfhood is realized.

What is interesting about these planks is that they fit together into a single worldview, a single way of looking at the world that can be used by people of different religions to interpret their respective points of view. Indeed, this bridge opens up the possibility that different religions have different ultimates, different features of reality around which they orient themselves. The Buddhist may orient his or her life around the impermanence and interconnectedness of all things as expressive of a deep creativity; the Jew may orient his or her life around a sense of covenant with God; and the Jain may orient his or her life around a non-violent approach to all living beings. From a Whiteheadian perspective, they have each discerned a truth of the universe. Each offers something to the larger whole of human experience by which humans can build multi-religious communities of the kind Gandhi envisioned.

2

A Walk in Beauty

A Process Approach to Peace between Religions

Hans Küng says that if there is to be peace in the world there must be peace between religions.[1] His reasoning is straightforward. The majority of humans are guided by religious outlooks on life, whether Hindu or Muslim, Jewish or Taoist, Christian or Confucian, Sikh or Jain, Buddhist or Bahai. When expressed in daily life, these outlooks can give rise not only to great beauty but also to great tragedy. This tragedy is especially obvious in the monotheistic traditions. A passion for what is changeless and permanent and pure, which many people experience as a passion for what they call "God," can lead people to build hospitals and orphanages; however, it can also lead them to fly planes into tall buildings and try to dominate others in the name of one true religion. The need in our time is for the world's religions to promote peace on earth and peace between religions.

But is "peace" the right word for what we humans seek today? Perhaps not. I recall a friend many years ago who declared half teasingly but half seriously that "peace is boring." He was struck by the fact that many people picture peace as a state of affairs that is calm, predictable, and lifeless. "One thing about violence," he said, "is that it gets your attention."

Of course, he was right about violence. When violence occurs, we are forced to either look at it or run away from it, but either way we are provoked. On the other hand, something even more troublesome is that the frenzy of violence can be interesting—indeed thrilling—for those who inflict it. This is one of the reasons that some men between the ages of eighteen and thirty find war so exciting. Training for war gives them a sense of meaning and purpose, allowing them to neatly divide the world into two opposing camps, good and evil, and to envision themselves on the side of good. Therefore, participating in acts of war, whether justified or not by moral standards, can make them feel like the gods of apocalyptic literature: holy warriors who inflict damage on enemies in the name of high ideals. Obviously, the victims of their violence, including the friends and family who are left behind, do not see things this way. One person's crusade is another person's hell. Nevertheless, in the act of inflicting violence, those making war can feel like gods. Violence can become an intoxicant.

Consequently, the question emerges: Once the political and social sources of violence are eliminated, can peace be intoxicating, too? Can peace be as enlivening in its way as violence is thrilling in its way? What might this more adventurous peace be like? In this chapter I want to offer an image of a more adventurous peace and then talk about ways in which peace between religions might contribute to it. Let's begin with the state of the world.

THE STATE OF THE WORLD

Imagine that a terrible catastrophe has occurred—a nuclear explosion or an ecological collapse—and that a parliament of world religions has been called to assess the damage and consider possibilities for hope. The participants recognize that, all things considered, the religions have been sources of tragedy as well as of hope. Therefore, they are not sure that their traditions are up to the task. On the other hand, the participants also recognize that something must be done by the religiously minded, because they constitute almost ninety percent of the world's population.

Imagine further that, by some strange twist of fate, we know someone who has been invited to give the opening address. Her task is daunting. She wants to speak in ways that will make sense to people of many different religions: Hindu, Muslim, Buddhist, Christian, Jewish, Jain, Shinto, Bahai, Sikh, Native American, indigenous African, and many others as well. She wants to be sensitive to the fact that they come from different social situations and cultural traditions and that they speak different languages, both linguistic and spiritual. She knows that she cannot speak for everybody and she is very glad to know that, after the opening address, people will divide into small groups where the many points of view can be presented.

However, someone must open the conference, and she must rise to the challenge. She wants to offer a word of hope, because she knows that some among the audience despair of the very possibility that religion has much to say to the world. But she wants to present an honest assessment of the state of the world lest anyone be deluded into a false optimism; she also wants to present some of the challenges that will be faced by people in the many world religions if they are to contribute to the world's well-being. What would we recommend that she say?

We could recommend that she read the preamble to the Earth Charter. It is a short document, created in the final decade of the twentieth century, which is now being used by educators around the world in schools and institutions of higher education as well as by community and professional development groups. Successive drafts of the charter were circulated around the world for comment and debate by non-governmental organizations, professional societies, and international experts in many fields. This means that it may embody the most inclusive process of global discernment the world has ever seen. It consists of a preamble and sixteen ethical principles, the most foundational of which is "respect and care for the community of life." The preamble reads as follows.

We stand at a critical moment in Earth's history, a time when humanity must choose its future. As the world becomes increasingly interdependent and fragile, the future at once holds great peril and great promise. To move forward we must recognize that in the midst of a magnificent diversity of cultures and life forms we are one human family and one Earth community with a common destiny. We must join together to bring forth a sustainable global society founded on respect for nature, universal human rights, economic justice, and a culture of peace. Towards this end, it is imperative that we, the peoples of Earth, declare our responsibility to one another, to the greater community of life, and to future generations.

Humanity is part of a vast evolving universe. Earth, our home, is alive with a unique community of life. The forces of nature make existence a demanding and uncertain adventure, but Earth has provided the conditions essential to life's evolution. The resilience of the community of life and the well-being of humanity depend upon preserving a healthy biosphere with all its ecological systems, a rich variety of plants and animals, fertile soils, pure waters, and clean air. The global environment with its finite resources is a common concern of all peoples. The protection of Earth's vitality, diversity, and beauty is a sacred trust.

The dominant patterns of production and consumption are causing environmental devastation, the depletion of resources, and a massive extinction of species. Communities are being undermined. The benefits of development are not shared equitably and the gap between rich and poor is widening. Injustice, poverty, ignorance, and violent conflict are widespread and the cause of great suffering. An unprecedented rise in human population has overburdened ecological and social systems. The foundations of global security are threatened. These trends are perilous—but not inevitable.

The choice is ours: form a global partnership to care for Earth and one another or risk the destruction of ourselves and the diversity of life. Fundamental changes are needed in our values, institutions, and ways of living. We must realize that when basic needs have been met, human development is primarily about being more, not having more. We have the knowledge and technology to provide for all and to reduce our impacts on the environment. The emergence of a global civil society is creating new opportunities to build a democratic and humane world. Our environmental, economic, political, social, and spiritual challenges are interconnected, and together we can forge inclusive solutions.

To realize these aspirations, we must decide to live with a sense of universal responsibility, identifying ourselves with the whole Earth community as well as our local communities. We are at once citizens of different nations and of one world in which the local and global are linked. Everyone shares responsibility for the present and future well-being of the human family and the larger living world. The spirit of human solidarity and kinship with all life is strengthened when we live with reverence for the mystery of being, gratitude for the gift of life, and humility regarding the human place in nature.

We urgently need a shared vision of basic values to provide an ethical foundation for the emerging world community. Therefore, together in hope we affirm the following interdependent principles for a sustainable way of life as a common standard by which the conduct of all individuals, organizations, businesses, governments, and transnational institutions is to be guided and assessed.[2]

To my mind, the paragraphs above represent a concise but accurate statement of the state of the world. Thus, they frame the context for considering the challenges faced by the world's religions today.

As explained in the previous chapter, I think that there are at least five of these challenges. Let me remind you what they are and amplify them a bit.

The first might be called the "Compassion Challenge," or the challenge to live lightly on the earth and gently with each other. This challenge is to identify teachings and practices within our traditions that are conducive to respect and care for the community of life, enabling us to help build communities that are just, participatory, peaceful, and sustainable. Facing this challenge involves two kinds of love simultaneously: first, listening to the needs of others, human and non-human alike, with sympathy and care, and second, responding to those needs in active ways, both personally and politically. Individuals and religious communities can respond to this challenge. One of the hopes of the world is that the many religious communities of our world will feel called, each in its way, to meet this challenge.

The second might be called the "Repentance Challenge," or the challenge to live humbly and self-critically. It is to acknowledge teachings and practices within our traditions that lend themselves to violence and arrogance, ignorance and prejudice. This challenge calls us to repent for these practices, adding new chapters to our religion's history in a spirit of ongoing conversion. Understanding and meeting this challenge can be facilitated by a study of the history of one's own tradition, seeing that it has from its beginnings been variable and changing. This confirms the recognition that religions themselves are dynamic and changing processes capable of growth and change.

The third can be called the "Simplicity Challenge," or the challenge to live frugally and simply while assuring that basic needs are met. Responding to this challenge in a creative way requires providing a meaningful alternative to the dominant religion of our time: consumerism. We can accomplish this not only by acknowledging the social and environmental costs of an overly acquisitive lifestyle but also by showing that life can be lived simply and joyfully, without falling into the tragedy of poverty or the trappings of affluence. The Earth Charter puts it well: "We must realize that when basic needs have been met, human development is primarily about being more, not having more."

The fourth can be called the "Ecological Challenge," or the sustainability challenge. Meeting this challenge means embracing an ecological outlook on life, recognizing that we are creatures among creatures, on a small but gorgeous planet, who have ethical responsibilities not only to other humans but also to the entire community of life. This requires accepting limits to economic growth, insofar as growth exceeds the carrying capacity of the planet and the capacities of local bioregions to absorb pollution. It also requires a deeper and fuller acceptance of mortality as part of the human condition. In the words of the Earth Charter, it requires "reverence for the mystery of being, gratitude for the gift of life, and humility regarding the human place in nature."

The fifth can be called the "Diversity Challenge," or the pluralism challenge. This is met by entering into friendships with people of other religions and promoting peace between religions not only for the sake of mutual understanding but also for the sake of mutual transformation, cognizant that each religion has something to teach the others.

THREE AIMS IN LIFE

The best hope for religion in our world is that religiously minded people respond to these five challenges in a constructive and creative way, relative to their objective circumstances and felt needs. People need not respond from a neutral or generic social location; they can respond as Confucians, Taoists, Hindus, Buddhists, Muslims, Jews, and Christians. Insofar as they do respond in creative ways, they bring hope to the world.

I use the word "hope" advisedly, cognizant that there are some who criticize the very word. I have activist friends who say that the best hope of the world is that people will stop hoping and get on with the task of living lightly on the earth and gently with each other. They say that there is too much hope and not enough action. And I have Buddhist friends who say that emphases on hope lend themselves to a frenetic way of being in the world, in which one can never be fully at home in the present moment because one is always on the way toward a happiness that never quite arrives. They add that this frenetic and willful way of living is itself one of the reasons the world can seem so hopeless. A better option, they say, is to give up hope and live compassionately and responsively, moment by moment.

Still, I hear a word of hope in their criticisms, and it seems to me that the word "hope" is unavoidable if we are to live responsibly and responsively. The better option, then, is to define the word carefully. In doing so, it is tempting to find a definition in terms of one or another of the world's religions. We might say that hope is the coming of the kingdom of God on earth as it is in heaven, or a collective awakening to the truth that everything is interconnected, or a recognition that the whole of the earth is a revelation of the divine mystery—a burning bush—for those who have eyes to see. But perhaps it is better to bypass the specific language of religion and turn instead to the poets.

Let us briefly return to Emily Dickinson. In the previous chapter, I noted that she speaks of hope as a small bird—a thing with feathers—that perches in the soul and sings a tune without words. The question emerges: How do we experience this bird that sings within us?

Here the philosophy of Whitehead is helpful. Whitehead proposes that humans and other living beings commonly live from three hopes: *to live, to live well,* and *to live better.*[3] To live is to survive physically. It is to have food on the table, clothing to protect one from the elements, and shelter from storms. To live well is then to survive with some degree of wholeness or happiness relative to the situation at hand. Buddhist mindfulness in the present moment would be a religious expression of the impulse to live well, as would an Abrahamic sense of awe and wonder in the presence of a beautiful creation. Finally, to live better is to enjoy fresh possibilities for thinking, feeling, and acting, avoiding a sense of staleness and brute repetition of the past. In the world religions, this would be exemplified in the hope for spiritual growth in this life—growth in wisdom, compassion, and freedom—and perhaps, a continuation of growth in an ultimate union of the soul with God or an ultimate awakening to the fullness of Truth. Of course, in human life, the third hope—to live better—can sometimes take the form of unlimited material acquisition. This is what happens in consumer culture when traditional hopes for wisdom, compassion, and freedom are replaced by hopes for a good appearance, affluence, and marketable achievement. The desire to have more replaces a desire to be more. In its worst aspects, consumerism builds upon the human desire to live well and better, turning it into something harmful rather than helpful.

In any case, Whitehead's three hopes help us understand how the bird is manifest in human life. The "thing with feathers" may be an indwelling lure within each living being to survive with satisfaction relative to the situation at hand and then, once needs for survival are met, to live in qualitatively rich ways in community with others, in ways that include openness to new possibilities. This would mean that when we hope for the fullness of life for ourselves and others—when we hope, in the words of the Metta Sutra in Buddhism, that "all living beings may be happy"—we are responding to a call that is very deep within life itself.[4] We are hearing the melodies of the thing with feathers and responding with melodies of our own. And when we act on these hopes, we are enabling the song to become incarnate in this world.

Are we alone in this holy endeavor? Whitehead implicitly proposes that even the universe is responsive to the song. Here he follows aspects of what is now taught in physics. Astrophysicists tell us that the universe is not a fixed and closed system that continually repeats itself like a loop in a computer program, but is instead an unfolding and unfinished process that actualizes novel possibilities over time. It is less like a machine than it is like an unfinished symphony or perhaps a jazz concert. Physicists then add that the world we see around us is a living testament to this creative process. The stars and galaxies, the hills and rivers, the people and penguins, the atoms and molecules are all products of a vast evolutionary process that has been unfolding over some fifteen billion years. Their present activities are adding chapters to the history of life, the history of the universe, adding new notes to the concert, such that, like music itself, the universe is different at every moment. They are created and creative co-creators, continually shaping a universe that is more like a pilgrimage than a destination. Perhaps then, the bird of which Emily Dickinson speaks is not simply biological or terrestrial but also cosmological. The bird may be an indwelling lure within the universe as a whole, inwardly animating each creature to seek its unique form of beauty and well-being and yet beckoning the whole of creation toward new forms of order that build upon inherited forms—living cells from molecules, for example, and then tissues from living cells, and then organs from tissues, and then people and penguins. The song of the bird may be the song of the universe.

Indeed, Whitehead implies that Emily Dickinson's bird of hope is God—or at least that aspect of God that is within the universe and within each living being as a lure to live and to live well. In using the word "God" to name the bird I do not mean that God is reducible to the hopes of human beings and other animals. We earthlings often create our own hopes and some of them seem quite out of sync with the larger song of the universe. Nor do I mean that the malevolent hopes of human beings—hopes for domination and control and vengeance—are the will of God. In naming the bird God, I do mean to suggest that there may be something deep and divine within each of us, calling us to realize our full potential. We experience this something not simply as a push from behind but rather as a pull from ahead, like being drawn by an invisible magnet. Like the song of a bird. Our calling as human beings is to hear the song and respond to it by actualizing new and hopeful possibilities in the current state of the world. It is to enter into a respectful way of living.

A WALK IN BEAUTY

How might we name this more respectful way of living? A process thinker would borrow from the Navaho and call it *walking in beauty,* then add some ideas from Whitehead, who is one of the few Western philosophers since Plato to take beauty as a defining feature of healthy living. For Whitehead, beauty is not simply an observable property of beautiful sunsets and melodious songs as seen with the eyes and heard by the ears; it is more deeply a property of how we feel and live in the world, day by day and moment by moment. Beauty includes our intentions and motivations, our attitudes and hopes, as well as more observable factors. Whitehead believes that in human life such beauty includes a walk in goodness and in truth. This means that when we walk in beauty we must listen to others and care for them, embodying what many call "goodness"; and it means that as we encounter ideas both new and old, we have the courage to entertain them freely and openly in response to the indwelling call of truth, which is itself a call to live in harmony—in resonance—with the way things truly are.

Of course, all of this sounds very human, so let us quickly recognize that, at least in Whitehead's view, beauty has many forms and human beings are not the only creatures who walk in beauty. Birds walk in beauty when they fly; fish walk in beauty when they swim; cats walk in beauty when they purr; humans walk in beauty when they love. All living beings have their distinctive forms of beauty, none reducible to the others and all adding to a diverse whole, which is beautiful in its variety. From Whitehead's point of view, the function of God within the evolutionary process is to elicit diverse forms of beauty of which other living beings, and even atoms and molecules and galaxies and stars, are expressions. Our vocation in human life is not to be lords of creation but to walk in beauty in distinctively human ways that add to, rather than subtract from, the beauty in the rest of creation. We are kin to the other living beings on our planet, and our vocation is to add beauty to the world, cognizant that the universe itself is, in the words of Thomas Berry and Brian Swimme, a communion of subjects and not a collection of objects.[5] The five challenges faced by the world's religions are simultaneously callings to add to the communion, to walk in beauty.

Are religious people up to the challenges? Are they up to the call? Certainly part of the process involves responding to the first two challenges named earlier: uncovering and highlighting resources for compassion—for respect and care for the community of life—that lie within our particular traditions; and simultaneously acknowledging and repenting for teachings and practices that lend themselves to violence and arrogance, prejudice and ignorance. The good news is that religious scholars who are examining the history of traditions and proposing fresh ways of thinking for the future are meeting these challenges today. Within Christian theology, for example, there are "liberation theologians," "post-colonial theologians," and "feminist theologians" engaged in construction and critique of their own traditions. Their counterparts exist in religious traditions such as Islam, Judaism, Hinduism, Buddhism, and many others.

Nevertheless, there are limits to a strictly scholarly approach, especially if it is separated from attention to the affective and attitudinal dimensions of life. Most of us who are drawn to walk in beauty know that its embodiment in our daily lives requires not only changes in outward behavior but also transformations of heart and mind, and we know that these transformations do not come about through scholarship alone. Our need is to find holistic ways of *being Muslim* and *being Christian* and *being Hindu* and *being Buddhist,* ways in which hospitality toward people of other religions, a willingness to live simply, and a welcoming of truth wherever it is found are as natural as singing songs and saying prayers. Somehow, the virtues of care and respect, of honesty and frugality, of hospitality and openness must become habits of our hearts.

For good or ill, these habits do not flow automatically from our beliefs or even our most cherished ways of thinking. We may believe quite fervently in love, for example, and yet not be very loving, and we may believe quite strongly in open-mindedness and yet not be very open-minded. We cannot simply will our way into respect and care for the community of life through the practical application of fervently held views or plausible convictions. A conversion of the heart must also involve a letting go—an internal surrender—to deeper rhythms of grace that lie within and beyond the human heart.

This deeper surrender can occur in many different ways. For religious people, it often involves and requires participation in a community of spiritual friends—in what Christians call *church* and Buddhists call *sangha* and Muslims call *umma*. If we seek to walk in beauty, we need to be "eldered" by friends who likewise seek to walk in beauty with open hearts. This is why healthy community is so important within and outside religion. It provides an opportunity for what Whitehead calls "empathy" or "feeling the feelings" of others such that we share in their "subjective aims" and "subjective forms" through experiences in the mode of "causal efficacy." The phrases are Whitehead's.[6] Subjective aims are purposes and intentions to which one is drawn as his or her immediate experience unfolds. They are aims to live, to live well, and to live better. Subjective forms are emotional tones that clothe a person's inner perception of the world. They are emotions such as anger and hope, fear and tenderness, confusion and clarity. Causal efficacy is the feeling of being affected, or influenced, by the experience of another. Whitehead's point, then, is that in listening to others and interacting with them, we are shaped by *their* subjective aims and forms, such that their feelings become part of *our own* lives. Their aims and feelings become our aims and feelings. Other philosophers sometimes speak of this empathy as *mimesis,* a sympathetic conformity to the outer behavior or inner conditions of others, such that their conditions have a causal influence on our own.

To be sure, mimesis, or shared subjectivity, can have destructive as well as constructive consequences. If we find ourselves in communities where insatiable desire—a wanting to acquire more and more material goods without ever having to say "enough"—is the norm, we can feel these feelings and be affected by them, such that those desires become our own. This is part of what happens in consumer culture. We feel the greed of others and we share in it. We become part of a community of desire, a society of greed. Something similar happens in religious communities where fear of strangers and rigid legalisms become the norm. We feel the fear of others and join in the fear ourselves. This is why, in addition to mimesis, freedom of thought it so important to healthy community. It provides an opportunity for individuals to gain distance from the more destructive aspects of shared subjectivity.

Still, shared subjectivity is critical to a walk in beauty, and if we are fortunate, we can share companionship with people whose own inner conditions involve an aspiration toward respect and care for the community of life. Because their feelings are contagious, we can sometimes catch those feelings. The habits of hospitality and openness then become our own, not because we will our way into them, but because we walk with others who are also trying to walk in beauty. Russian Orthodox Christianity puts it well when it says: "One can be damned alone, but saved only with others."

The needed transformation of the heart can occur in still other ways. For example, it can occur through the natural world when we are awestruck by the sheer complexity and beauty of other forms of life. In such moments, we experience what might best be called "green grace," that is, a kind of healing that can occur only through a recovery of felt bonds with the earth and sky, with plants and other animals. Nature itself becomes our teacher and healer, our primary revelation. The emergence of respect and care can also occur with the help of spiritual disciplines such as meditation and prayer, dancing and fasting, which often touch the deeper recesses of the human heart where creeds can never go. Almost always, the transformation can emerge in the context of helping others.

Often, when we truly give time and energy to help others in direct and palpable ways, we discover that, as a by-product, something opens wide in our own hearts that otherwise might remain closed. We are saved not by seeking happiness for ourselves but by helping others become happy.

In short, a walk in beauty can be facilitated not only by theology but also by the companionship of others, a recovery of felt bonds with the earth, a practice of spiritual disciplines, and service to others. In whatever way the walk emerges in our lives, it emerges not simply as an achievement but also as a gift: something that happens to us and in us, apart from our more willful ways of being in the world. The psychiatrist Gerald May puts it well when he says that a walk in beauty involves a spirit of willingness as opposed to willfulness: cooperating with something deeper and wider and richer than the private self.[7] Most of us who are religious know that a walk in beauty requires such willingness, such cooperation, so that our attitudes and awareness can be transformed. It is only with changes in attitude and awareness that people can become the peace that they so often commend to the world.

THE FIVE CHALLENGES REVISITED

Let me summarize what I have said so far. I have suggested that, given the state of the world, the world's religions face five serious challenges: to live compassionately, to live self-critically, to live simply, to live ecologically, and to live with hospitality toward other religions. I have said that there is a "thing with feathers" within each human being that can help that person respond to these challenges and that the thing with feathers is God. I have also suggested that a response to the five challenges best takes the form not simply of a theological approach to life but still more deeply of a walk in beauty, an entering into a willing approach to life as deepened by companionship with others, the green grace of the earth, prayer and meditation, and loving-kindness. Through ideas such as these, I have tried to introduce process theology.

Another way to introduce process theology is to note the way it might respond to religious objections to the five challenges named earlier. In presenting the challenges earlier, I recognized that my very framing of them is contestable and that some will disagree with them on religious grounds. Here are some possible objections.

Obedience is more important than compassion. There are some who would say that a call to compassion is less important than a call to obedience, because the true purpose of the religious life is not to "love thy neighbor" but rather to make peace with divine beings or departed ancestors for the sake of security and prosperity in this life or the next. Others of a more mystical bent might say that it is to be absorbed into a sense of oneness with ultimate reality, in light of which the problems of the world are seen as unreal.

My religion contains no imperfections. There are some who believe that the teachings and practices of their own religion are timelessly perfect and not subject to correction, such that it would be blasphemous rather than pious to suggest that the teachings need changing or that one's own religion is capable of improvement.

Consumerism is fine. There are many in the world who believe that consumerism is perfectly compatible with the practice of their religion, who ignore traditional injunctions to live simply, who believe that "greed is good" because it contributes to a growing economy, and who equate personal wealth with godly living.

The earth is for human use alone. There are some who believe that an ecological outlook on life is sinful rather than praiseworthy because it comes close to worshiping the earth, which is finite and does not deserve worship. They also believe that the earth and its creatures exist only for human use.

My religion is better than all the others. There are many for whom friendship between religions is undesirable because they believe that only their religion contains insights relevant to salvation.

Added to these objections, there is still another objection that might be articulated as: *It's all in God's hands anyway.* There are some who believe that the whole of the world is governed by a divine power from whose perspective the future is already decided, so that no decisions humans make in the present can alter or change the already-determined outcomes of worldly events. They feel that the very idea that religious people are "called" or "challenged" to respond to immediate situations, thus contributing to an undecided future, is deluded, because the fate of the world unfolds according to a script that is already clear in God's mind. The better option is simply to trust that things will unfold as they are supposed to unfold, quite apart from our presumptions concerning how we might influence the future.

Process theology responds to each of these objections by presenting an alternative point of view. Process theologians believe (1) that human beings are called by God to live compassionately and that such compassion—understood very broadly as respect and care for the community of life—is the deepest form of obedience; (2) that we are likewise beckoned by God into a life of collective self-criticism such that no achievements of the historical past, including those embodied in inherited teachings and practices of our own religion, are immune from criticism; (3) that we are called to live simply and joyfully, avoiding the trappings of affluence as well as the tragedies of poverty so that there will be enough for all; (4) that we are called to recognize and appreciate the value that other living beings have in and for themselves, quite apart from their usefulness to us; and (5) that we are called to welcome, rather than fear, religious diversity because all religions, not just one, contain wisdom conducive to the flourishing of life. For process theologians, the universe is a creative and creating process of interdependent events, lured but not controlled by God, such that the future is not yet decided, not even by God. This means that, if the will of God is to be done "on earth as it is in heaven," God needs and requires human cooperation.

Finally, and most important, process theologians do not think that responsiveness to the lure of God in life requires the use of the word "God" or the envisioning of God in personal terms. An interesting feature of process theology is the recognition that linguistic experience is but the tip of the experiential iceberg and that the words we use to name our deepest and most legitimate hopes and callings, and the ideas we employ as compasses for our lives, are important but not absolute. If we affix ourselves to them too rigidly, we make gods of them and fall into a kind of verbal idolatry. Moreover, the indwelling lure of God may itself beckon each of us to name and envision things—even God—in different ways, such that there is not a single "right way" to think or speak. All of this is to say that the small bird of hope—the thing with feathers—can be named in many ways. The bird of hope may indeed call some to say "The Lord" and some to say "The Abyss" and some to say "The Universe" and some to say nothing at all.

Whatever we might name the bird of hope, one thing is clear. If its will is to be done on earth as it is in heaven, there must be peace between religions. In the remainder of this chapter, I want to offer a Whiteheadian approach to such peace.

THE CASE AGAINST RELIGION

There was once a time, not too long ago, when many secularly minded people believed that peace on earth would come as a result not of peace between religions but of an elimination of religion altogether. Many of these critics were Westerners and they often equated "religion" with what they knew of Judaism, Christianity, and Islam. They were troubled by aspects of the Abrahamic religions that lend themselves to violence, intolerance, ignorance, and arrogance. They were wary of the claims so often voiced by Christians and Muslims that their religions are superior to all others because they contain the only truth required for salvation.

These secular critics believed and hoped that more secular ways of thinking would come to prevail in our world. This would happen through economic development, as a result of which people would gradually, and perhaps unconsciously, lose their more traditionally religious ways of thinking. In a post-religious world, so the critics believed, science would provide the knowledge needed for wise decision-making; technology would provide the goods for a comfortable life; economics would provide the means of producing and distributing the goods. The inherited teachings of the world's religions—the Four Noble Truths of Buddhism, the Good News of Jesus, the Five Pillars of Islam—would come to be seen as failed attempts to transcend the conditions of finitude. And the longings that sometimes gave rise to such teachings—the longing for reconciliation with God or awakening to ultimate reality—would be supplanted by more mundane but meaningful concerns, such as having a good job, having good friends, and enjoying opportunities for recreation and leisure.

Given the power of religion in our world today, these predictions concerning an end to religion seem outdated. Muslims and Christians combine to form almost half the world's population, and their numbers are growing. In Europe and North America, the third great missionary religion, Buddhism, is very much on the rise. All over the world, local communities embody ways of living that are "religious" in one way or another. This suggests that if religion is a disease within the human heart, it is an incurable disease, hardwired into the human brain through centuries of evolutionary adaptation.

Nevertheless, there is some truth in the secularly minded predictions, because in our time many religious people have been converted, wittingly or unwittingly, to a certain kind of secularism. I call it "consumerism." It is arguable that the two most powerful influences in our world today are Western-based consumerism and the religion of Islam, each competing with the other for the hearts and minds of billions of people all over the world.

By consumerism I do not mean consumption. I do not mean having food, clothing, and shelter or enjoying simple but

meaningful pleasures. I do mean (1) an over-consuming lifestyle that is characteristic of about one-fifth of the world's
population and envied by many others and, more important,
(2) an attitude toward life and a set of values that validates
and valorizes such a lifestyle. To understand these attitudes
and values, we can imagine them as forming a world religion
not unlike the way in which Confucianism, for example, con-
stitutes a world religion. Confucianism does not have a cen-
tralized bureaucracy, but it is indeed a way of thinking and set
of values in which many East Asians share. It emphasizes respect for elders, allegiance to the family, a fulfillment of social
responsibility, and social harmony. It is the traditional way of
thinking in East Asia.

Consumerism, then, is Confucianism-in-reverse. It is also a
set of values, but it emphasizes youth over age, career over family, and pleasure over community. Its god is economic growth; its
priests are politicians and economists who understand growth
and promise access to it; its evangelists are advertisers who dis-
play the products of growth and insist that people cannot be
happy without them; and its church is the shopping mall. It
promises salvation, not by grace through faith as Christians
claim or by a dropping away of the ego as Buddhists claim, but
by appearance, affluence, and achievement. Its doctrine of creation is that the earth is real estate to be bought and sold in the
marketplace; its doctrine of human existence is that we are
skin-encapsulated egos whose highest good lies in accumulating
wealth and material possessions. Insofar as these ways of thinking are promulgated twenty-four hours a day through radio and
television, they have tremendous influence on the human psyche,
quite apart from the issue of religious affiliation. People may
think of themselves as "Christians" or "Muslims" or "Buddhists" or "Jews," but if we were to observe how they spend
their time, energy, and money, we might find that many of them
in fact center their lives on consumer-driven values. To the degree that they have centered their lives on these values, a quiet
but effective conversion has occurred. They are religious in
name and attitude, even to the point of fighting others in the

name of their religion, but they are secular in lifestyle and personal values. For the evangelists of secularism, a victory has occurred. Religion has been replaced by consumerism.

Would this victory be all bad? If there is a God who calls the peoples of the world toward peace, justice, and sustainability, would this God lament the fact that people are more focused on appearance, affluence, and marketable achievement than on more lofty matters such as "grace" and "redemption" and *"nirvana"*?

Perhaps not. To be sure, secularism has its social and environmental costs. The historical record shows that purely secular societies—like Maoist China and Stalinist Russia—can be as violent, if not more violent, than religiously based societies. And a secular state can be as ecologically destructive and politically repressive as any theocracy. Still, consumerism can seem harmless when compared to forms of religion that give rise to injustice, arrogance, violence, superstition, narcissism, ecological destruction, intolerance, the exploitation of the poor, the exploitation of women, and a stifling of human creativity. Sometimes religious devotion does lead to these ills. When this happens, simple consumerism can seem to offer better possibilities. It is understandable how some people believe that the best hope for human life is not that people say "I am Christian" or "I am Buddhist" or "I am Muslim," but rather "I am a member of the Pepsi Generation."

Most religious people, and I count myself among them, resist this suggestion. We sense that there is something wise in the teachings of the world's religions, and there is something spiritually shallow, if not also ecologically destructive and socially harmful, in consumerism. We would rather live from wisdom, compassion, and freedom than from appearance, affluence, and achievement, and we believe that religions at their best help induce wisdom, compassion, and freedom. Accordingly, we seek not an end to religion but a transformation of religion so that it can provide a meaningful alternative to consumer-driven values and thus better serve a world in need. The five challenges faced by the world religions point to needed areas of transformation.

Religiously minded people are called to live compassionately, to live self-critically, to live simply, to live ecologically, and to promote peace between religions. The challenge to live self-critically is especially important, because religions can sin and indeed can serve as conduits for original sin. Let me explain.

RELIGIONS AS CONDUITS FOR ORIGINAL SIN

Can religions become evil? Charles Kimball thinks so. As a student of religion and violence, Kimball proposes that religions become evil when: (1) they claim to have the only path to God, (2) they claim to have the only way to read a sacred text, (3) they encourage blind obedience to religious leaders, (4) they focus on apocalyptic ends to history, which they themselves will help bring about, and (5) they are willing to use destructive means to achieve religious goals.[8]

These are simply warning signs. Of course, they are not sufficient in themselves to produce violence. They must be ignited by other conditions such as economic marginalization and political frustration, exaggerated pride and debilitating humiliation. But when the other conditions are in place, the warning signs become kindling for the destructive fires expressed in violence between religions, violence committed in the name of religion, or violence inflicted on others with the implicit sanction of religion.

Process theologians in the Christian tradition take a step further and suggest that when religions become violent, they simultaneously become sinful. Here, the work of one process theologian, Marjorie Suchocki, is especially helpful. By sin, she does not mean rebellion against God as if God were a monarch whose primary concern is to be flattered. Rather, she means unnecessary violence against creation, the effects of which are felt and suffered even by God. Sin is "unnecessary violence against any aspect of existence, whether through act or intent, whether consciously chosen or otherwise."[9]

If we accept Suchocki's definition of sin as unnecessary violence, we can see that there is a great deal of sin in the world.

Sin includes sexual abuse, cruelty to animals, neglect of the elderly, racial prejudice, the wanton destruction of forests, the denial of food to the hungry, terrorism, the denial of rights to women, and the over-consumption of material goods on the part of consumer society. Most, if not all, of this violence is unnecessary.

However, in defining sin as unnecessary violence, emphasis must be placed on the word "unnecessary," because life requires some degree of violence, as witnessed in predator-prey relations and also in the simple act of eating. If humans are to survive, we must eat, and eating itself involves the taking of one life, like that of a plant, in order to sustain our own life. This is why Suchocki defines sin as *unnecessary* violence. Acts of sin are acts of violence that, all things considered, should be and could be otherwise.

Suchocki helps us make sense of the idea of original sin. In saying "original sin," she does not mean a primordial act of disobedience committed by Adam and Eve, the consequences of which are inherited by future generations. Rather, she means tendencies toward sin with which people are born, even if they do not consciously or willingly choose those tendencies. Suchocki's research suggests that some of these tendencies are inherited genetically, as illustrated in impulses toward aggression that once served important evolutionary purposes, but are now counter-productive to the living of life, and others are inherited from the cultures into which a person is born, as illustrated in impulses toward prejudice that may be a part of a person's culture. Her point is that we are not born as blank slates, devoid of impulses toward good and evil. Rather, we are born with conditions and into situations that shape us from the very beginning, both for good and for ill. Quite apart from our intentions, we often fall into violence by virtue of these inherited and socially induced tendencies.

Thus, acts of sin—that is, acts of unnecessary violence— can emerge from the conscious and willful intentions of their perpetrators, exemplified in conscious and willful acts of cruelty, but they can also emerge unintentionally, and sometimes unconsciously, without the perpetrators having intended them.

A young boy who is born into a culture that hates Jews or Muslims or Christians is born into a form of sin that he does not choose but that can shape his life. He is born into original sin. Only with personal effort and with the help of a community that introduces him to a less violent way of living in the world can he transcend this sin and add beauty to the world.

Moreover, acts of sin can be committed not only by individuals but also by communities of individuals, including cities and nations, corporations and professional organizations, cultures and religions. Religions can be vessels for great good in the world, but they can also be vessels for great sin. Indeed, despite their tendencies to the contrary, religions can be carriers of original sin. They can be conduits by which tendencies toward violence are passed from one community to the next and one generation to the next.

Of course, religions themselves are abstractions. They do not act as agents in their own right; instead, they are ways of thinking and feeling and acting embodied in various ways by various human agents who can act violently. The phrase "religion can sin" is shorthand for "certain religious ways of thinking and feeling and acting lend themselves to sin when appropriated in certain ways and when other factors are in place." It is the people, not the religions, that sin. Still, the religions can lend themselves to sin when their ways of thinking foster unnecessary violence of any sort, whether it is violence between religions, violence committed in the name of religion, or violence inflicted on others with the implicit sanction of religion. Hans Küng is right in one of the key theses of his global ethic: there cannot be peace in the world until there is peace between religions.

PEACE AS BEAUTY-IN-THE-MAKING

We best begin by defining "peace" not simply as the absence of violence but more deeply as the presence of the fullness of life. And let us also recognize that this fullness can be felt in varying degrees and ways not only within individual human beings as they enjoy a personal sense of well-being but also between people as they enjoy rich relations with one another. Peace is not simply inner serenity; it is also the give and take of mutually enhancing relationships. Of course, some of these rich relations are intimate and personal. They include the poignancy and creativity of satisfying relations between spouse and spouse, parents and children, friend and friend, lover and lover. When these relations are mutually enhancing, there is a meaningful taste of interpersonal and intimate peace. Much of the world's great love poetry and much of the world's greatest music are embodiments of, and serve, this intimate peace.

But peace also includes rich relations of a more public and political kind, and politically concerned people rightly resist a reduction of the world to strictly intimate terms. Peace is what happens when people participate in the decisions that affect their lives. It is *democracy*. Peace is also what happens when people's basic needs for food, clothing, shelter, health care, and education are met and when they have opportunities for meaningful and satisfying work. It is *justice*. And peace is what happens when people live in harmony with the earth and other living beings, making space for the whole of life to flourish. It is *ecological well-being*. This more political side of peace is like a three-legged stool. Its platform is respect and care for the community of life and its three legs are justice, democracy, and ecological integrity. Many people in our world today are working hard for this kind of peace in one of its three aspects. They speak of peace as a just and sustainable world.

In addition to these two dimensions of peace—interpersonal peace and political peace—let us also recognize that peace can include a more mystical or ultimate side. Peace can include an inner, or subjective, journey toward what Buddhists might call "the enlightened life" and Christians might call "life in Christ" and Muslims call "the surrendered life."[10] These phrases name a deeper and more complete side of peace, which, according to most world religions, all humans long for consciously or unconsciously as we seek satisfying personal relations and as we struggle toward just and sustainable communities. A Buddhist would

say that there is a Buddha-nature within each of us—a potential for enlightenment—that is partially realized in healthy
friendships and harmonious communities but that can be fully
realized only when we wake up to the pure presence of things
as they truly are. A Christian would say that there is an empty
space—a God-shaped hole—that can be only partly filled in satisfying relationships and just communities but that can be completely filled only by the presence of God. A Muslim would say
that there is a deep and hidden memory within each of us—an
awareness of God—that can be awakened when we see that the
whole of the universe is a sign of God but that can be finally
tasted only by a dropping away of the self so that only God remains. If these intimations of an ultimate peace make sense,
then it is obvious that most people on our planet die without
ever having fully experienced it. Indeed, and unfortunately,
many die without having experienced even small approxima-
tions of interpersonal or political peace. In thinking about
peace, it is important to recognize that the journey toward
peace may extend after death in a continuing journey toward
what Buddhists call final *nirvana* or Muslims might call para-
dise or Christians might call everlasting life.[11] The possibility
of this final peace is important, not because death itself is a
problem, but rather because so many people die without realizing any semblance of peace. The problem is not death; it is in-
completeness.

So far, I have recommended that we define the word "peace"
as the fullness of life, known in varying ways and degrees and
capable of being experienced at three levels: interpersonal, political, and mystical. In making these claims about peace, I realize that, at least for some readers, I may be defining peace in
more dynamic and relational terms than are customary. If you
are among these readers, I ask you to be patient with me, because I want to suggest that peace is worth seeking in this life
and perhaps even in the next life. It is worth *knowing*. By
"knowing," I do not mean indirect knowing, like knowing the
recipe for freshly baked bread. Rather, I mean experiential
knowing, as when we taste the bread itself with our very own
tongues and enjoy it. Or, if the metaphor of eating is too palpa-

ble, perhaps we might compare peace to music that we are enjoying in a live concert.

When we "know" music in a live concert, our knowledge comes not from reading the score but from hearing the rhythms and melodies and being absorbed in them, enjoying their sonorous effects. If someone asks us why we like the music, we could say that it sounds "good" or "true" and then add that these values, goodness and truth, are ends in themselves and desirable in their own right. But we would probably appeal to the third Platonic value—beauty—and simply say, "It is beautiful, and that's why I like it." And this, I think, is one of the true attractions of peace. It tastes good and feels good. It is pleasurable. It is beautiful in a healing way.

In our time, it is important to emphasize the pleasure of peace if only to provide an alternative to the pleasures of violence. After all, people who are drawn to violence often find it strangely beautiful, albeit in a destructive way. This is why it functions as an intoxicant. They are drawn to violence as a moth is drawn to a flame even if, when they approach the flame, it kills them.

If peace is to be enlivening, it must be equally, if not more, attractive. Here Whitehead can help. He defines *beauty* as a meaningful synthesis of two qualities of experience: *harmony* and *intensity* (PR 279). Harmony is what we feel when we are at one with other things; intensity is what we feel when we are filled with creativity and zest. The problem with boring peace is that it is harmonious but not intense; the problem with unnecessary violence is that it is intense but not harmonious. From a Whiteheadian perspective, a more adventurous peace will be both harmonious and intense, neither to the exclusion of the other. It will be like an improvisational jazz concert: beauty-in-the-making.

In picturing the more political side of this beauty, we need not envision a unified world order that is harmonious in every respect or that is governed by a single imperial ruler. We need not picture a world that is controlled by the United States of America, or by a consortium of transnational corporations, or by a culture of religious clerics, or by the culture of consumerism.

Nor need we picture a utopia in which humans are utterly free from loss and pain, having arrived at a state of perfect ease in which the whole world has become a euphoria of artificial pleasures. There is something good and natural—indeed beautiful—about the human condition with all its frailty. But perhaps we can picture local communities in different parts of the world—Islamic, Asian, African, American, and European—that are characterized by meaningful degrees of respect and care for the community of life. The relevant image of communities is not that of heads of state at international conferences posing for photo opportunities. It is that of people of different religions and of no religion traveling on the same buses, working together, playing together, and sharing civic responsibilities for the sake of a common good.

In order for these kinds of communities to emerge, education is critical. People need to be equipped with the practical skills of business and agriculture, science and technology. They need tools for living. But they—we—also need to be schooled in the moral skills of listening and forgiveness, gratitude and humility. This is especially the case for those of us who are religious. Somehow Muslims, Christians, Jews, and Hindus need educators who can help them understand that "being a Muslim," "being a Christian," "being a Jew," and "being a Hindu" means, among other things, being a good listener and forgiver. Religious leaders must seek resources within their own traditions for listening and respect, and they must embody these resources in the very ways of living. They must follow Gandhi's example; they must *become* the peace they commend to the world.

Of course, the moral virtues of listening and forgiveness, respect and compassion are not enough. Peaceful communities also require the trans-moral virtues of laughter and celebration, ritual and ecstasy. A peaceful society will need a spirit of playfulness and ease; it will need to be fun and even funny if it is to be satisfying and sustainable. It needs people who can laugh with each other and at themselves because they have learned to let go of pretenses to perfection, including pretensions to having arrived at perfect peace. In this regard, religious traditions that encourage humor as a mode of spirituality—Judaism and Zen Buddhism, for example—have a particularly important role to play in cultivating the art of peace. They can help lighten the load of inordinate sobriety. Zen Buddhism does this, for example, through its use of stories of Zen Masters which, among other things, often involve humorous antics revealing the spontaneity of the Zen life in the here-and-now of each present moment; Judaism does the same through its use of stories that so often include a spontaneous capacity of rabbis to poke fun at one another and, in some instances, at the very Master of the Universe, who seems also to enjoy a good laugh.

Above all, though, a peaceful community needs to be creative. An adventurous peace will not have the passive quality of a painting, the forms of which remain fixed as observers come and go. Rather, as noted above, it will be like the continuous creation of an improvisational jazz concert, in which the musicians are essential to the music. The dynamics of peace are similar to a creative and evolving harmony of sound, created by different musicians, each with his or her talents adding something to the larger whole. Their interactions can be unpredictable and surprising; there will be moments of tension, and there will be times when the concert threatens to dissolve. Still, among the musicians, there will be a commitment to keep the concert going, not only because fidelity to the bonds of relationship is good in its own right but also because there are times in the concert when the musicians feel so completely alive that they can never imagine violence as a preferred alternative. The challenge in our time is to grow into this aliveness.

3

God's Fondness for Beetles

A Process Approach to God, Creativity, and the Sacred

> *Glory be to God for dappled things—*
> *For skies of couple-colour as a brinded cow;*
> *For rose-moles all in stipple upon trout that swim.*

—Gerard Manley Hopkins

When asked what he had learned about God after a lifetime of studying nature, the British biologist J. B. S. Haldane allegedly said, "I have learned that God has an inordinate fondness for beetles."[1]

If Haldane said this, he would have had a good point. Beetles have inhabited our planet for some 250 million years. Humans have been on earth for only a few hundred thousand years. There are least 350,000 species of beetles on earth, which amounts to a quarter of all known animal species. This suggests that God may have not just a fondness for beetles but perhaps an unusual, divine obsession with them.

Of course, if Haldane did make the remark, he would have been speaking facetiously. He was known to be skeptical of theistic religion, and his remark would have been designed to poke fun at theists who unwittingly assume that God is a human-like deity residing several miles off the planet whose entire purpose in creation was to create human beings. This would mean that fifteen billion years of galactic history and five billion years of earth history were designed for only one purpose: humans. A question naturally emerges: If humans were the sole purpose of galactic and biological evolution, why did God wait so long? Why not simply begin with humans and simultaneously create the rest of the universe for their enjoyment?

Haldane is known for another quote as well, which also bears upon an understanding of God. The universe, Haldane said, is not just stranger than we imagine, but stranger than we *can* imagine.

A healthy religious life must include what one science writer, Ursula Goodenough, calls a *covenant with mystery* if it is to avoid the idolatry of making a god of its own beliefs and pretending a certainty it lacks.[2] In the spirit of Haldane, we might even speak of a covenant with strangeness.

By strangeness, I mean the sheer mystery that there is anything at all where there could be nothing. Whitehead speaks of this mystery as the depths in the nature of things, alluding to it in the first part of *Process and Reality,* where he writes: "There remains the final reflection, how shallow, puny, and imperfect are attempts to sound the depths in the nature of things. In philosophical discussion the merest hint of dogmatic certainty as to finality of statement is an exhibition of folly" (PR xiv). A covenant with strangeness includes recognition that any sounding of the depths eludes finality of statement.

By strangeness, I also mean something a little closer to home. I mean the subjective worlds of other living beings whose ways of feeling the world may be very different from our own but may nevertheless be beautiful. Here, I use the word "beauty" in a Whiteheadian sense. I mean harmony and intensity of subjective feeling.

Beetles would be a good example of this second kind of strangeness. From a process perspective, they are indeed subjects of their own lives and not simply objects of human observation, because they feel the presence of the world around them and respond in their unique ways. In the language of process theology, they have "intrinsic value" and not simply "instrumental value."[3] And yet, their subjective worlds must be very different from what we humans know.

Consequently, one might ask what it means to say that beetles are subjects. It does not mean that they exist in isolation from their environments or from the surrounding world but that they feel the presence of their world from subjective points of view. In process thought, conscious experience is but the tip of the experiential iceberg beneath which lie many other forms of experience that are subconscious but powerful.

What, then, is consciousness? By consciousness, process thinkers mean a particular kind of experience or, more accurately, a certain way of experiencing the world characteristic of the ordinary waking consciousness of animals with sufficiently complex nervous systems. This way of experiencing includes a sensation of clarity combined with an intuitive awareness that what is clearly present could be otherwise. We can experience ideas clearly, and we can also experience the world around us clearly, as is the case in much conscious visual experience. Process thinkers add, though, that most of our own experience lacks this clarity and awareness, and by implication, most beetle experience will likewise lack it. Beetle experience may well be vague, dim, and subconscious and, by virtue of a beetle's body chemistry and social environment, very strange by human standards.

But strangeness lies in the eye of the beholder. If beetles are aware of humans in a conscious way, we can only imagine that from their point of view we humans would be the strange ones. Moreover, if we abandon all caution and playfully imagine that beetles have something like theistic religion, we can only trust that, for them, God will be an omnipresent Beetle in whose image all beetles are made. By virtue of their numbers and longevity, beetles could legitimately argue that it is they, not we, who have dominion over the earth, and that it is they, not we, who have been most faithful to God's commandment to be fruitful and multiply.

Of course, imagining the world from a beetle's point of view is fanciful and some might ridicule it as irrelevant to any real concerns. But from a process perspective, such an imaginative exercise is, in its own way, a kind of prayer, because it is a way of sharing in the divine life. In process theology, God is immanent within all living beings as a lure to live with satisfaction. God knows not only humans but also non-humans with an incomparable intimacy. God does indeed know what it is like to be a beetle, even though humans can have only a dim intuition. Accordingly, a playful meditation on "what it might be like to be a beetle" can be a spiritual practice in its own right, a finite and human sharing in divine empathy for each and every creature. Equally important, such imagining can be a healthy antidote to a kind of anthropocentrism that too often, and unnecessarily, creeps into monotheistic consciousness. We monotheists all too frequently imagine the earth as a castle of divine making, designed for human use and pleasure, with the rest of creation as mere backdrop. Process theology recommends a more ecological perspective, one in which God is pictured as including, not excluding, the whole of creation.

What, therefore, is God in process theology? In order to explain, I must first offer a process approach to the Sacred. Of course some people equate God and the Sacred, and certainly there are many contexts in which, given certain definitions, these words can and should be used synonymously. Nevertheless, when we speak of what is extremely important to us we often say "It is sacred to me," even as we are not claiming that the object of our appreciation—a friendship, for example—is identical with God. An interesting feature of process thought, then, is that it encourages us to recognize that, in the history of religion as in ordinary life, there are several realities which, in different contexts, people can experience as sacred. Some explanation is in order.

FOUR FACES OF THE SACRED

Many scholars of world religions understand the religions as finite attempts, emerging through trial and error over thousands of years of biological and cultural evolution, to experience something called the Sacred. Functionally, the word "Sacred" refers to anything that is experienced as irreducibly real or trustworthy, thereby eliciting a sense of awe or respect. Given this definition, process theology proposes that in the history of religions there are at least four realities that are rightly experienced as irreducible in their respective ways, and around which different peoples can center their lives: the Abyss, the All, the Divine, and the Present Moment. We might speak of these as four faces of the Sacred. Each face is ultimate in its own way, and each elicits a distinctive kind of spirituality that is complementary, and not necessarily contradictory, to the others. While many if not most people experience several of these four faces simultaneously, we can also explain them separately. First, the Abyss.

By "the Abyss" I mean that bottomless well-spring of creativity which is expressed in whatever happens as it happens, whether tragic or comic, violent or peaceful, healthy or unhealthy. Whitehead calls this reality Creativity, and in the first chapter I treated it as one of the twelve key concepts on a Whiteheadian bridge between religions. In passing I noted that it is analogous to what some Buddhists mean by *sunyata*, which is a creative emptiness that is expressed in every formed reality, and also to what some Chinese philosophers mean by *ch'i*, the spontaneous and continuous activity of the earth and heavens.

Considered in itself, then, this Abyss—this pure activity—is not a creator god but is instead the self-creativity of each and every being—terrestrial or celestial, earthly or galactic, visible or invisible, angelic or demonic, human or divine—as it spontaneously responds to its surroundings. Understood in this sense, the Abyss is neither good nor evil, pleasant nor unpleasant. It is the is-ness of what is. It is the sheer activity of a person loving another, but also the activity of a person harming another. It is the hunger of the fox as he chases the rabbit and also the fear of the rabbit as he flees the fox. It is the power of a cancer cell to replicate itself in the brain, and also the power of the brain trying to withstand that replication. It is the hatred of the warrior as he seeks to exterminate his foe, and it is the compassion of God as God shares in the suffering of all, including the warrior's foe, seeking the well-being of all. As the happening of what happens, the Abyss is not a transcendent reality if by transcendent we mean something that has agency of its own. And yet it is deep and inexhaustible, like a bottomless well of creativity that is manifest anywhere and everywhere, at every time and all times. Mystics in different parts of the world are rightly awed by the depths of this Abyss and in certain moments of their lives they awaken to its depths, realizing that all beings, even divine beings, are expressions of it. It is no accident that in some Western traditions it is called the Godhead: the groundless ground of which the personal God is an inclusive, self-creative expression.

Nevertheless, not all religious people are interested in the Abyss. Many are more interested in what we might call the All: that is, the totality of finite beings throughout the universe that exist in reciprocal relation to one another. The All is itself the Abyss, but in traditions that emphasize the totality, the emphasis is placed not on the depths of creativity but rather on the interconnected and web-like nature of creation itself. Thus the All is everything, understood as a vast network of inter-being or inter-existence. For many people, this network is known most intimately not as an abstract concept in the mind but rather as the immediacy of reciprocal relations within a particular community, whether the community is a tribe or clan, a church or *sangha*, a nation or rainforest. Traditions that are centered in the All are not especially concerned with mystical awakening to the Abyss or to an ultimate reality. They understand spirituality in terms of fidelity to the bonds of local relationship with human community and with the earth. For them the Sacred is in the relationships themselves, and more specifically in reciprocal relationships. When asked what is ultimate or sacred, they will not say "the Abyss" but rather "the Connections."

On the other hand, people in monotheistic religious traditions usually orient their lives not around the Abyss or the All but rather around a single Divine Reality, understood as embracing the universe or presiding over the universe, whose will is directed toward the well-being of finite creatures. In the philosophy of Whitehead this Reality is named God, and it is conceived as the primordial expression of the creative Abyss who embraces the entire web of life within a general horizon of love. If we imagine the Abyss as an underlying ocean that is manifest in all the waves of the ocean, then God is an inclusive wave, a Wave that embraces all the other waves, holding them in its embrace. All the waves taken together—the finite waves and the inclusive Wave—then form the All.

Understood in this way, God has agency and self-consciousness of God's own, which means that God has aims and purposes for the world, aims that may or may not be realized. Whereas the Abyss is the happening of what happens, whatever happens, God is that Reality in the universe which embraces the universe as a whole, helping guide it into happenings that are creative, healthy, beautiful, and just. In this sense God completes the Abyss, giving it purpose and direction. In the language of Whitehead, God is the primordial manifestation of Creativity.

I will say more about God shortly, but for now it is important to note that there are some traditions—Zen Buddhism, for example—that emphasize not the Abyss or the All or the Divine but rather the ultimacy and irreducibility of each present moment, understood as that place where the many of the universe become one in the spontaneous happening of what happens. In Whiteheadian terms these traditions take concrescence itself, as described in chapter 1, as the ultimate reality. In these traditions, the point of life is to be fully present in the moment, to be fully alive and responsible to the call of the moment. Of course the advocates of these traditions may affirm cosmological notions such as the Abyss or the All or the Divine. They may emphasize that the most authentic way to be present in the moment is to be grounded in the Abyss, or awakened to the Totality, or trustful of the Divine. Nevertheless, what is most important to them is not an apprehension of these ultimates as objects of intellectual understanding but rather the act of living in the moment itself, cognizant that each moment is an ultimate reality that cannot be reduced to the past or the future. In the Christian tradition, for example, this tradition is expressed in the idea that the heart of Christianity is not to attain a happy afterlife, but rather to practice the presence of God in the sacrament of each present moment. In the practice itself, as embodied in the immediacy of each moment, God is present.

Let me summarize my thesis so far. It is that in the history of religion there are at least four faces of the depths in the nature of things, or, as we might also put it, four faces of the Sacred: the Abyss, the All, the Divine Reality, and the Present Moment. Process theologians typically use the word God to name the divine Reality. From a process perspective, the Abyss is the ultimate reality, itself manifest in each present moment and also in the totality of existents, and God is then ultimate actuality: that all-inclusive and self-creating form of the Abyss whose nature is unbounded love, and who seeks to guide other beings into forms of self-creativity that are healing and whole-making.

This emphasis on Creativity as the ultimate reality is important both religiously and scientifically. Scientifically, it means that evolution itself is a creative process, both in its galactic dimensions and in its biological and cultural dimensions. It also means that this Creativity is not reducible to the choices of a single, divine creator. The results of evolution may be tragic or happy, beautiful or horrible; either way, they are creative. Religiously, an emphasis on Creativity means that there can be forms of spiritual experience that are centered in Creativity rather than in God, and that these forms of spiritual experience have wisdom in their own right, with or without God. Many process thinkers believe that Buddhist awakenings to Emptiness and Hindu awakenings to *Nirguna Brahman* are of this kind. In these awakenings, something ultimate is seen which is not God. Equally important, the emphasis on Creativity helps process thinkers deal with the question of God and tragedy. There is tragedy in the world that God will not and cannot prevent and that is tragic even to God. Here, a further word about God is in order.

ONE-EMBRACING-MANY

With most monotheists, process theologians believe that God is One. However, in the spirit of Haldane, process thinkers recommend that we begin our thinking about God's oneness with a recognition that we live in a large and strange universe, filled with billions upon billions of galaxies, in which we humans are small but included.

Our task is then to imagine God's oneness as something that embraces or contains the universe. God is One-embracing-many. More specifically, God is a universal consciousness—everywhere at once—who is equally present to each and every creature: to the smallest of sparrows on Earth and to the most distant of black holes. Indeed, God encircles the universe, which means that the universe is inside God, not unlike the way in which fish are inside an ocean or embryos are inside a womb or clouds are inside the sky. This does not mean that everything that happens in the universe is willed by God. Just as embryos within a womb have creativity that is not reducible to the mother, and fish in the sea have creativity that is not reducible to the ocean, so things happen in the universe that are not reducible to God or God's will. Horrible things happen that cannot be prevented by God and that are tragic even to God. Children are murdered; women are raped; animals are abused; forests are needlessly destroyed. Still, the universe is inside God, and it affects God at all times.

The implications of this perspective are significant. If we believe that the universe is inside God, this means that when we witness terrible tragedies that inflict horrible suffering on living beings, the tragedies happen to God even as they happen to the living beings that suffer. And it means that when we look lovingly at another human being or we gaze in awe at the multicolored textures of beetles, we are seeing part of what makes God "God." The universe is God's body. Not a sparrow falls without God being moved. God is the unity of the universe—the larger whole, in which the universe unfolds.

This larger whole can be felt but not grasped because we are always inside it. It is not "this object" or "that object" or even "all of them added together." Rather, it is that in which all living beings live and breathe and have their being. Many of us sense this larger whole—this One-embracing-many—when we gaze into the sky on a dark and starlit night. Just as the dark sky is not a star among stars but rather encompasses all the stars and the earth as well, we sense an encompassing wisdom that is not an entity among entities within the universe but rather a womb-like mystery that embraces the heavens and the earth. This reality is what process thinkers have in mind when they say "God." They mean One-embracing-many.

ONE-WITHIN-MANY

They also mean One-*within*-many. In process thought, the spirit of God is also within each creature as its innermost lure to live with satisfaction relative to the situation at hand. And, in a general way, the spirit is also the counter-entropic lure that, despite the tendencies of energy toward chaos, has drawn the universe to create new wholes from pre-existent parts. Atoms come from subatomic events, molecules from atoms, stars from molecules, galaxies from stars and, at least in life on earth, living cells from molecules, tissues from living cells, organs from tissues, and then bodies, and so on. This does not mean that galactic or biological evolution is the result of a pre-existent design on God's part but that God lures the universe into self-creating new forms of order relative to what is possible in the situation at hand. Evolution is an ongoing process, not yet finished, that is prompted, but not coerced, by the indwelling spirit of God into newness.

The idea that God is within living beings can help us understand how religion emerges in human life. In human life, this divine breathing takes many forms. Certainly, it is within each of us, as our own innermost lure to live with satisfaction, expressed among other ways in our simple will to live. When we see people struggling to survive against difficult odds in situations of poverty or warfare or abuse, we see the presence of God in them. The divine spirit animates their spirits, and they are responding in the most natural of ways, creatively adapting to the situation at hand. Biologists tell us that this creative adaptation serves an evolutionary purpose, increasing the chances that their genes will survive in new generations. Process thinkers will add that, even if their genes do not survive, the creative adaptation has value in its own right, moment by moment. God is in creative adaptivity.

In process thought, the lure of God within each human life is not only a lure to live but also a lure to live well, to live with beauty—with harmony and intensity—relative to the situation at hand. In other words, the indwelling lure of God within each human life is not only an inner impulse to creatively adapt to new situations; it is also an impulse to seek the good, to be open to what is true, and to celebrate what is beautiful—all of which are forms of creative adaptation. Some outward expressions include the creation of music, the enjoyment of friendships, the cooking of food, the search for knowledge, the telling of stories, the pursuit of justice, courage in suffering, and befriending strangers. The lure of God within human life takes many forms, all making the whole richer.

At their best, the world's religions are responses to this indwelling lure to live well. On the one hand, they are embodiments of a human struggle to survive with satisfaction, and some of their strategies may involve *useful fictions* that facilitate that survival. For example, if a world religion teaches that "we have the only truth," this teaching may serve as a means by which people in the religion promote their own survival and help assure the prospects of future generations of believers even as the teaching contradicts the divine lure toward goodness. Just because an idea is conducive to survival doesn't mean the idea is right. The idea may be wrong but useful.

In this book, of course, I am assuming that the world's religions involve more than useful fictions. Over time, and through trial and error in response to the divine lure toward truth, they have uncovered wisdom worthy of universal appreciation. In this sense, all religions are partly inspired by God, just as all science and all art are partly inspired by God. Not only the lure to survive but also the lure toward wisdom is a deep and ineradicable dimension of the human heart, and religion contains part of this wisdom.

It is important to emphasize, though, that divinely inspired wisdom in religion does not need to be about God in order to be wise and important. Buddhists, for example, are especially wise about the impermanence of all things, which is itself "ultimate" in its own way. Without awareness of impermanence, we humans cannot be saved from our excessive clinging to finite things—sometimes quite beautiful things—that inevitably pass away in time. Buddhists rightly tell us that our clinging usually leads to great suffering and sadness, not only in ourselves but also in others upon whom we foist our projections of permanence. The wisdom of Buddhism is saving, not because it points to God who saves us but because it helps us make peace with impermanence. It can help us live more lightly on the earth and more gently with each other.

To offer another example, many indigenous religious traditions in Africa, Asia, and the Americas are remarkably wise about our kinship with other creatures. More than most of the classical and text-based traditions, the indigenous traditions often emphasize that we humans are part of a wider community of life that includes other creatures. This does not mean that indigenous traditions always treat other creatures in a friendly way. No human traditions have a monopoly on ecological wisdom. But it does mean that indigenous traditions typically recognize, more than others, the importance of establishing reciprocal relations with the extra-human world. In this sense, they help us realize, in the words of Thomas Berry and Brian Swimme quoted earlier, that the universe itself is a communion of subjects and not simply a collection of objects. Thus, the wisdom of indigenous traditions is saving, not because it points to a saving God of the kind emphasized in Abrahamic religions but because it points to an attitude that can save us from ecological collapse.

ONE-BETWEEN-MANY

So far, I have said that, from a process point of view, God is One-embracing-many and One-within-many. It is important to add that God is also One-between-many. By this, I mean that God is not only beyond each living being and inside each living being but also between all living beings, inasmuch as living beings dwell in mutually enhancing relationships.

This emphasis on mutually enhancing relationships raises a profound question for all theists, process theists included, as they attend to certain aspects of biological life, specifically predator-prey relations. The question is fairly simple: If God is a lure toward wholeness within each living being, whose side is God on as the fox chases the rabbit?

The process view is that God is on the side of each: luring the fox to find the rabbit, since it is the only way that the fox can survive, given his or her genetic dispositions, and luring the rabbit to escape the fox, given that it is the only way for the rabbit to survive as well. This can mean that God is deeply pained by the relationship, precisely because it is not mutually enhancing, since one individual must be frustrated. Or it can mean, as many environmentally minded thinkers might prefer, that God is in the relationship itself, as a necessary way for life to unfold on earth.

The first response is one way that process thinkers would make sense of the idea, found in the Christian tradition and also other traditions such as Jainism, that nature itself has a tragic dimension that falls short of pure harmony. The second response is a way in which process thinkers make sense of the idea, found in many traditions, that there is somehow something beautiful in nature, including predator-prey relationships because, even in their violence, they reveal a deep and necessary interdependence by which one living being feeds another. I see wisdom in both points of view, yet neither is entirely satisfactory. Violence in the world, necessary or unnecessary, cannot be reduced to something that makes sense. In the last analysis, it is beyond rational explanation, and yet we must accept it as part of life without pretending that we fully understand why it occurs.

In any case, many of the world religions find something sacred in mutually enhancing relationships. In indigenous traditions, as noted above, human-earth relationships can be mutually enhancing. And in many of the classical religions, something very special and even sacred can be found in human-human relationships, as in Jewish emphases on collective fidelity to the bonds of covenant, in Confucian emphases on the primacy of family life, in Buddhist emphases on *sangha* (community), in Christian and Muslim emphases on developing trans-cultural and trans-ethnic communities of believers. In many traditions, the key to mutually enhancing relationships lies in empathy, which is experiencing the feelings of others in acts of loving-kindness. The prophetic traditions then add that such relationships also include justice, understood as fidelity to the bonds of relationship. In a more personal and intimate vein, Christianity adds further that one of the most sacred relationships, which is itself a lesson in love, is marriage.

A process approach to God is sympathetic to all of these emphases because it finds God in relationship, particularly when relationship involves empathy and loving-kindness. It then adds, as do several religious traditions, that God calls humans into expanding circles of empathy, beginning with family but reaching out to include many others, human and non-human, in horizons of care. As humans respond to this call by dwelling responsibly and lovingly in community, they make the Divine Reality still more visible on earth. In Christian terms, the word or spirit of God becomes flesh not only within individual hearts and lives but also in community. This is one reason that peace on Earth—including peace with the earth and peace between religions—is so important. Peace enables God to become more fully incarnate in the world.

THE MANY TRUTHS OF THE WORLD'S RELIGIONS

What can we humans do, then, to help God become more incarnate in the world? One way is to undertake friendly readings of the many world religions, helping to create a culture of peace. A friendly reading is not a naive reading. We can undertake friendly readings of other religions, as well as of our own, with full awareness that religions can become evil: that is, that they can be conduits for violence and prejudice, arrogance and ignorance. A friendly reading simply realizes that the dark side of religion is not the whole story, and religions like human beings contain wisdom as well as foolishness. A friendly reading is interested in affirming the truth in each religion.

A process approach to world religions recognizes that the many religions contain at least three kinds of truth: truthful belief, truthful awareness, and truthful living.

Truthful belief lies in the entertainment of religiously relevant ideas which are true—or at least seem true—to the person who entertains them. Whiteheadians emphasize that no idea is absolutely or unquestionably true, because all ideas are shaped by human finitude. Even the ideas that God is One or that everything is interconnected or that we are kin to other creatures are finite and fallible because we inevitably entertain and articulate such ideas through a lens of social construction and cultural conditioning. They are relatively true in the sense that they have pragmatic value, helping us move through life relative to different contexts, and they are relatively true in the sense—so we hope—that they have some resonance with the depths of reality. Still, we can never know with certainty that they have such resonance, because there is always more to these depths than our minds can fully fathom. Truthful belief need not be certain belief. It can instead be trustful belief that relinquishes certainty in the interests of humility. Indeed, a smug sense of certainty can actually be the enemy of truthful belief because it masks the fact that truth is always more than our concept of it. When it comes to truthful belief, process thinkers say, we should hold our beliefs with a firm, yet relaxed, grasp.

By truthful awareness, I mean something different from truthful belief. I mean states of consciousness—feelings and moods and perceptions—that reveal some aspect of the truth that lies in the nature of all things. An example of truthful awareness would be Buddhist mindfulness in the present moment, in which a person sees what is happening without projecting "beliefs" onto the situation or adding further commentary. In this instance, the truth is simply the situation as it is. Buddhists call this the "such-ness" or "as-it-is-ness" of what exists. They see truthfully when they see mindfully, and they can help us do the same. Another example of truthful awareness is a sense of kinship with fellow creatures found in so many indigenous traditions that try to live in reciprocal relationships with the larger web of life. These feelings are not reducible to beliefs about the plants and animals as if a conceptual judgment needs to be made in order for the feelings to be true. Rather, the truth lies in the feeling of kinship, like that experienced by indigenous people who exist in sympathetic conformity with the energies of the plants and animals that surround them. A third example of truthful awareness is the feeling of awe and mystery that can be found in many monotheistic cultures when people intuit the encompassing reality of a divine Mystery who is both infinitely distant and infinitely near. As we stand beneath the heavens on a dark and starlit night, feeling small but included in a larger whole, we intuitively feel a sense of awe and mystery. We know something about the way things are, not through formal beliefs but through deeper feelings.

From a process perspective, such forms of awareness are truthful because they are truly attuned to the way things are, albeit in a finite way. They are revelations in which something that was concealed becomes unconcealed and is now known in an intuitive way. But they are not propositional revelations contained in verbal formulas or doctrines. They are deeper than words and they reveal a world beyond words. As we seek to listen to and learn from other religions, we need to be sensitive to these kinds of truthful awareness. Our friendship with people of other religions cannot simply be a comparison of belief systems. We must be sensitive to the feelings and intuitions of others, trusting that, with effort and deep listening, we ourselves might be able to take part in those experiences.

The same kind of sensitivity is needed in relation to truthful living. Such living has to do not with what people say or

even perceive but with how they live their daily lives in relation
to the world. Often such living incorporates insights that have
been acquired in practical and hands-on ways rather than
through private reading or through a reception of verbalized
messages. The insights emerge, as it were, from body to mind
rather than from mind to body. Oftentimes, such body-to-mind
insights emerge through ritual, as is illustrated in the Jewish observance of Sabbath and the Muslim observance of daily prayer.
In observing the Sabbath, the observant Jew sometimes comes
to feel that there is indeed a spirit of rest and relaxation—of
inner and outer peace—that is the very presence of God in
human life. After sundown on Saturday, when the Sabbath is
over, he or she may then tell you that the truth of the Sabbath
is best known not in talking about the Sabbath after the fact
but in observing the Sabbath habitually and with reverence.
The truth is in the action. The same applies to Muslim prayer.
In the act of prostrating oneself before God in the company of
others, the observant Muslim sometimes discovers a divine
unity that embraces everyone, regardless of race and social
class. After praying, the Muslim may tell you that the truth of
prayer *(salat)* is in the act of praying, including its bodily dimensions. In other words, the experiences of standing shoul-
der-to-shoulder and kneeling down together cannot be fully
understood simply by reading a book.

Of course, for many Jews and Muslims, and for many in
other religions as well, the ultimate form of truthful living does
not lie in ritual behavior but in ethical activity, expressed in acts
of respect and care for one's community. The sermon of one's
life is not in what one says or even in how well one performs a
given ritual but in the way one lives in relation to others.
Gandhi understood his own life to be an ongoing experiment in
truthful living, and he emphasized that the truth of his life lay
not in what he said but in how he treated others.

For some Christians, the same applies to Jesus. When they
say that Jesus is the Way and the Truth and the Life, they are not
referring to the beliefs about reality that Jesus entertained, much
less to the beliefs that people may have had about him. Rather,
they mean the truth of how he lived, moment by moment, in

submission to the calling of God. Christians such as these come to appreciate the Muslim and Jewish view that Jesus was a man among men who sought to enact "the will of God on earth as it is in heaven." As a Jew, Jesus would have been surprised to learn that several centuries after his death, some of his followers would emphasize right belief over right action. Jesus also seems to have been more interested in orthopraxis than in orthodoxy—that is to say that he was more interested in truthful *living* than in truthful *believing*. It is hard to imagine him creating theological fences that shut people out. His aim was to tear down fences so all might be included.

In making these comments concerning truthful living, my purpose is not to belittle the significance of belief. I want to emphasize that truthful belief is but one form of truth, and that healthy religion also involves truthful awareness and truthful living. As we facilitate peace by honoring the wisdom of other religions, it is important to recognize that wisdom has many faces. For so many people in our world, the most important forms of wisdom are not reducible to truthful belief. The truth is in the experiences of emotion and action.

TWO KINDS OF LEARNING:
MIND-TO-BODY AND BODY-TO-MIND

In a Whiteheadian context, an interest in truthful awareness and truthful living is rightly accompanied by a recognition that, in many forms of religion, the discovery of truth can occur through two forms of learning: learning from mind-to-body and learning from body-to-mind. An example may help.

Once a year, I teach a course called "State of the World" to college undergraduates. Its purpose is to provide graduating seniors with an overview of the world situation, including the problems of violence identified above, and also to invite them to consider their vocational options in light of the state of the world. One feature of the course is that it is also a *service-learning* course, which means that students are required to do five hours of volunteer work a week as a complement to classroom discussions. Their volunteer work includes activities such as harvesting crops at a local organic farm, playing basketball with at-risk youth, and preparing meals at a shelter for battered women.

From the Whiteheadian perspective, service-learning activities such as these make good educational sense because human beings can learn not simply from mind-to-body but also from body-to-mind. Mind-to-body learning is what occurs in the classroom where my students and I typically sit in chairs, relatively indifferent to our bodies, focusing on the ideas that come from written texts and open-ended discussion. Of course, we bring our bodies with us, but they remain in the background of our awareness as if they were ancillary to the process of learning. Our focus is on the ideas, and we are trustful that the ideas, if valid, can be "applied" outside the classroom in more bodily ways. In the classroom, we are living, for the most part, in our heads.

Body-to-mind learning is what happens in the service-learning component of the course. My students find themselves engaging in a variety of hands-on activities, possibly giving rise to insights they might not otherwise have. Body-to-mind learning also plays an important role in many world religions, including Western religions that find wisdom in liturgy and Eastern religions that find wisdom in mediation. It is a kind of learning that Whitehead's philosophy is especially sensitive to because his philosophy places a great deal of emphasis on what he calls "experience in the mode of causal efficacy," which consists in feeling what is happening within one's own body and being shaped by what is felt. For him, this kind of experience has been too often neglected in modern Western philosophy with its emphasis on visual experience of external objects as the primary example of perception. For Whitehead, perception also includes empathic perception as well as kinesthetic perception, which occurs when we experience the movement of our own bodies and are influenced by that movement.

Zen meditation provides a good example of kinesthetic perception. Meditation proceeds by placing the body in a balanced and restful state and then attending to the rhythmic process of breathing. Thus, the body becomes foreground rather than the background in the immediacy of experience. The idea is that a quiet body can yield a quiet mind. The "quietness" of this mind is not that of sleep or trance; it is a state of relaxed yet alert attention, in which one is aware of the pure presence of things as they are, without judgment and without any attempts to control them. In time, Zen Buddhists believe, familiarity with this mode of consciousness can assist a person in listening to other people on their own terms and for their own sakes, without reacting to what they say with judgments of one's own; and it can assist a person in listening to the earth itself.

Of course, in teaching State of the World, I do not require Zen meditation, though often I have wished that my students had a little more relaxed yet alert attention. But I do indeed presume that there is wisdom that can emerge through the body and that a neglect of bodily experience is a liability of overly intellectualized forms of learning. Moreover, if we wish to reduce violence in the world, people of different religions must do things together in bodily ways that serve the purposes of peace. In facilitating peace, kneeling together in prayer, sitting quietly together in silence, or working together to till an organic garden can be as effective as considering matters of doctrine. A Whiteheadian strategy for peace between religions involves religious people doing things together, learning from each other and also from the bodily action, especially if the action if is of a healing and constructive nature.

I must add that no forms of truthful belief, awareness, or living are absolute or final or sufficient unto themselves. There is always more depth than anyone's experience can grasp; therefore, one needs a covenant with mystery. I must also add that the divine lure toward wisdom within human life is simultaneously a lure toward beauty—a beauty that is more than wisdom. As indicated earlier, beauty is not so much a property of objects in space as it is a property of the soul and of individuals in community. It is satisfaction—happiness, if you will— that is inwardly rich and that is outwardly expressed in respect and care for one's community. It occurs in many degrees and many ways. From a Whiteheadian perspective, the lure toward wisdom within human life is part of a deeper lure toward beautiful living, which includes the beautiful soul in community with a wider world. Islam calls this kind of beauty *ihsan* and recognizes it as a central dimension of the surrendered life. A Whiteheadian would agree, adding that there are many forms of *ihsan*.

MANY SALVATIONS

The many kinds of experiential salvation offered in the world's religions—*moksha* (Hinduism), *nirvana* (Buddhism), *wu-wei* (Taoism), the *hallowing of life* (Judaism), and *life in Christ* (Christianity)—can best be understood as forms of beauty or forms of harmonious and intense experience to which individuals and communities can awaken. I stress "experiential" salvation because, in certain forms of Christianity, salvation is understood as an ontological status given to an individual or community, quite apart from what they experience. It is a metaphysical status, not a felt reality. In a Whiteheadian context, however, the felt reality of salvation is most important, and this reality is relative to the truths in which there is awakening. The truths are "saving" insofar as they help yield these various forms of satisfaction. For example, insofar as a person feels forever restless and not-at-home in the present moment, the Zen recognition of the pure presence of things as they are is indeed saving. Awakening to this pure presence yields the kind of satisfaction sought. And insofar as a person feels that his or her humanity is being denied in the present—through racial oppression or domestic abuse or a host of other injustices—then an awakening to the fact that things can be different in the future is likewise saving. Both of these experiences are guided by a subjective aim of beauty, by a desire not only to live but to live happily with qualitatively rich satisfaction. And with this common guidance, both experiences lead to different kinds of satisfaction, each of which has its distinctive tonality.

The question emerges: Are some forms of satisfaction compatible with, or even conducive to, violence? At this point a

Whiteheadian approach joins a Gandhian approach and says, "No, not if they are genuine forms of salvation." It is imaginable, for example, that a religious group will awaken to the truth of the self-structuring creativity of each present moment, and that it will recognize that this truth is, in its own way, neither peaceful nor violent, such that it can unfold either way. From a Whiteheadian perspective, this would be an example of truthful belief and also truthful awareness. It is true to say that there is a difference between peace and unnecessary violence, beauty and sin, and that freedom can unfold either way. However, in a Whiteheadian context, conformity to this fact through violent acts in the world is not itself saving because it diverges from the divine lure toward beautiful living, which is a lure toward non-violent living. In other words, truthful living has a certain priority over truthful belief and truthful awareness.

In a Whiteheadian and Gandhian context, truthful living has many forms relative to the truths to which people have awakened, but these forms are complementary to one another; one truth does not exclude the other. For example, one of the "truths" to which many religions awaken is that each living being has value in and for itself even apart from its usefulness to others. With its emphasis on *ahimsa*, Jainism is keenly sensitive to this truth and is centered on it, but other religions point to this truth as well, as in Jewish emphases on the goodness of creation and indigenous emphases on other living beings as spiritual kin to humankind. There seems to be an intuition that other living beings matter, that they count, because they are subjects of their own lives and not just objects for humans and other creatures. In Kantian terms, they are ends in themselves and not simply means to other ends.

Many forms of salvation are compatible with one another even if different from one another, and they are simultaneously compatible with the truth of intrinsic value. For example, a mystic who awakens to the undifferentiated unity of the divine mind, filled with potentialities which may or may not be actualized in the universe, has awakened to a truth—an extremely important one. But this truth does not exclude the complementary wisdom of the theist who apprehends the divine reality as a Thou to whom he or she is present in prayer. Both are "saved" by their respective forms of wisdom, and both forms of salvation are compatible with, even if not focused on, the truth of intrinsic value. However, unnecessary violence—sin—neglects this complementary quality. It involves an exercise of freedom in ways that violate the intrinsic value of other living beings and contradicts the "truth" of this value. If a way of living is truthful, it will not violate or contradict intrinsic value. If people in a given religion claim that God commands them to kill others (non-human and human alike) in God's name, they are mistaken about God, who is the indwelling lure toward truth. If they believe that they are saved through killing, they are likewise mistaken about salvation. Salvation has many forms, but sin is not one of them.

A CONTINUOUSLY CREATIVE UNIVERSE: INSIGHTS FROM CONFUCIANISM

We return to the question: How can any meaningful degree of peace come about on our small and fragile planet? An important feature of the Whiteheadian approach to peace is that it recognizes that peace has both an inner and an outer dimension. On the one hand, peace involves the journey of an individual life toward peaceable selfhood, experienced through one or another form of salvation. On the other, it involves human beings dwelling in community with others in ways that are harmonious and intense. Each participant is on his or her own individual journey, but that journey includes, and is partly composed of, the very presence of the others. If we use the word "alone" to describe the individuality of participants, then the participants are alone together, and their aloneness includes togetherness.

In a philosophy of complementary pluralism, the world's religions have important insights into both dimensions of the journey. In order to illustrate the applicability of a Whiteheadian approach to the communal dimension, it helps to bring Whiteheadian thinking and Confucian thinking into dialogue. This is because, with its emphasis on person-in-community as opposed to person-in-isolation, its recognition of the power of empathic awareness, its emphasis on harmony in society, and its deeply ecological nature, a Whiteheadian approach to peace bears similarities to Confucianism; one can easily imagine a Confucian Whiteheadianism, in which the richness of Chinese insights is combined with, and adds to, the power of the Whiteheadian approach.

Of course, "Confucianism" is an abstract name for many ways of thinking that have evolved in China, and it is difficult to make too many generalizations. But numerous interpreters of Confucianism suggest that peace—understood here as harmony in society—is built not only by government but also individual by individual, family by family, household by household, and community by community. Confucianism teaches that peace requires the cultivation and expansion of empathy, through which a person is able to imagine himself or herself inside the shoes of another, understanding that person's subjective aims and intentions, moods, and motivations. This empathy best begins in small ways, with siblings getting along with siblings, spouses with spouses, and friends with friends. Only as they become the peace they commend to the world does peace emerge. One Confucian scholar, Mary Evelyn Tucker, characterizes this extension of empathy when she observes: "A useful image for describing the Confucian ethical system is a series of concentric circles with the person in the center. In the circle closest to the individual is one's family, then one's teachers, one's friends, the government, and in the outer circle the universe itself."[4]

To this image of concentric circles Confucianism adds the practice of empathy or respectful relations—what Confucianism calls *li*, or as it is sometimes translated, manners. Here the word "manners" does not mean something stiff and lifeless but something gracious done for the sake of whole relationships, such as writing thank-you notes, shaking hands when greeting someone, or addressing an older person in an honorable way that acknowledges the wisdom of experience. These simple acts are part of the culture of peace—the way in which people learn to get along with each other, respect each other, and learn from each other. In their quiet and seemingly simple ways, they are rituals by which the deeper patterns of the universe—the widest aspect of the concentric circle—become ingredients in daily life. They are examples of the "body-to-mind" learning described above, showing how bodily activities can express deeper ritual patterns that belong not only to human cultures but also to the earth community from which human cultures emerge.

Of course, even at the small and local levels of peace, people who seek peace ought not to expect utopias. No amount of hand-shaking or thank-you notes can bring about the messianic age. Family life bears this out. Sometimes the forms of peace that are most difficult to sustain are those between family members, and more than a few ambitious souls have avoided the trials and responsibilities of family life by pouring their energies into what they take to be "larger" concerns, such as careers and participation in the public sphere. Those left behind become responsible for peace within the domestic sphere because the breadwinners are never at home. Nevertheless, there may be a blessing for those responsible for the domestic sphere and also a curse for those who do not participate in it. It is the homemakers of the world—female and male alike—who are in a particularly good position to learn the arts of empathy and thus the arts of peace. Moreover, it is important to point out that the private and public spheres of life are mutually influential, such that attention to the private sphere requires attention to the public sphere.

All of these reflections bear upon a Whiteheadian approach to peace. A process approach agrees with Confucianism, and also with Judaism, Islam, and countless other family-sensitive traditions, in emphasizing that genuine peace cannot and ought not exclude the domestic sphere. It also agrees that this peace can be facilitated in bodily ways, through the exercise of ritual practices—*li*—that promote the arts of peace. Yet a process approach also agrees with feminists and with victims of domestic abuse, including women in Confucian and other settings who have experienced the oppression and tediousness that often come from being solely responsible for domestic life. In order for peace within households to emerge within families in which women and men live together, there must be mutual respect and shared responsibilities. If any semblance of peace is to emerge in our world, relations between the sexes must be mutually enhancing, and much of this begins in the sphere of family life.

However, it is important to add that a Whiteheadian vision of peace, like a Confucian vision, does not end with family life, and it does not even begin with family life to the exclusion of other points of departure. Rather, it begins by paying attention to all the concentric circles simultaneously, from the personal to the political, the local to the global. At the same time, it involves sensitivity to the divine dimension of reality: to the One-embracing-many—the divine embrace. And it involves cognizance that the universe itself—the many that are embraced by the One—is itself a web of unfolding connections. This is not always a happy web or a peaceful communion, but it is a communion in the sense that each creature contains all the others.

In order to appreciate this deeper web, Confucianism is again helpful. The aim of life, so Confucians say, is to become fully human, and part of this process involves sensitivity to the fact that reality is a single and dynamic whole, consisting of a trinity of heaven, earth, and humanity. Equally important, all dimensions of this interactive whole—the heavenly no less than the earthly—are expressions of a deeper reality that is sometimes described in Chinese thought as *ch'i*. In Chinese philosophy, *ch'i* has many connotations, but it often means something like, in the words of a leading Chinese scholar, Tu Weiming, a continuously unfolding creativity or "spontaneous self-generating life process" that is manifest in all things, including departed ancestors, hills and rivers, human beings, water and plants, and divine realities.[5]

A Whiteheadian approach to peace agrees with all of this. The Whiteheadian cosmology presented in *Process and Reality* encourages us to imagine the universe as multi-planed, including a heavenly as well as an earthly dimension; it recognizes that all living beings, in whatever plane of existence, are subjects, not objects; it recognizes that no subject exists by it-self because all are internally related to all others; and, as developed by process philosophers and theologians, it finds plausible the possibility, deeply affirmed in so many world religions, that the larger peace may well include harmonious relations with departed ancestors who dwell in non-visible planes of existence. It then adds, as would many East Asian and South Asian traditions, that these non-visible planes need not be understood as supernatural, interrupting the laws of physics and chemistry. The whole of nature—including heaven, earth, and humanity—is the trinity.

Process thinkers build on this natural trinity by adding a more contemporary emphasis on creative evolution, suggesting that nature is an evolving process in which, over time, there emerge new things that have no parallel in what came before. This invites recognition not only of Confucian Whiteheadianism, but also of Confucian Darwinism, in which further emphasis is placed on the emergence of novelty in the continuously creative process of the universe. In life on earth, for example, there was once a time when single cells did not exist and had never existed except perhaps as God's ideas. But, some four billion years ago, single cells emerged as creative products of natural processes. The same applies, of course, to plants and animals, including human beings. This emphasis on nature as a process that is evolving, not only on earth but also in its galactic dimensions and perhaps also in the non-visible planes of existence that parallel our galaxy, leads Whiteheadians to imagine peace as a dynamic and creative process rather than a settled and static fact. Peace includes novelty as well as stability, intensity as well as harmony, and its ultimate aim is beauty. With its emphasis on family, empathy, harmony, and *li*, Confucianism shows how this peace can be concretized in the public and visible dimensions of daily, communal life.

To this emphasis on life in community, however, one must add an emphasis on the more private dimensions of a journey toward peace. In a Whiteheadian context, this inner dimension involves seeking meaningful degrees and kinds of satisfaction in daily life, in community with others who likewise seek meaningful degrees and kinds of satisfaction. It involves a quest for beauty, the ultimate expression of which is what many religions call "salvation."

I have previously said that many religions point toward different kinds of salvation relative to the different problems that humans can face and the different truths to which humans awaken as they grapple with these problems. A Whiteheadian perspective helps us appreciate both the unity and the diversity in these kinds of salvation, and it also helps us appreciate the possibility that the journey toward deep satisfaction continues after death.

In a Whiteheadian context, all forms of salvation are forms of satisfying existence—or forms of beauty. As indicated earlier, beauty within the soul refers to two experiential qualities that are sometimes separated but that can be combined: harmony and intensity. In the course of a lifetime and even a day, harmony and intensity are evanescent, but in their evanescence they form the very spice of life. Harmony is what we feel when we have lunch with a friend and enjoy a good conversation, and intensity is what we feel when, in the middle of the conversation, something hilarious or deeply meaningful is shared. Harmony is what we feel when, after a long day, we are able to go to sleep, and intensity is what we feel when, in sleep, we are awakened by an earthshaking dream. Harmony is what we feel when we are reconciled with someone from whom we have been estranged, and intensity is what we feel when, having reconciled, we pour our energy into a common task. In all of these instances, the harmony has some degree of intensity, and the intensity has some degree of harmony. Somehow, says Whitehead, it is in the coalescence of these two qualities that life becomes beautiful. And beauty requires the passage of time, including the death of what was once beautiful, for it to occur at all. If reality were frozen, if human life did not flow, moment by moment, there would be no beauty.

This does not mean that, in the flow of life, there cannot be enduring patterns of beauty. Many human beings understandably want and need harmony and intensity in stable yet fluid forms. Sometimes this is expressed as an inwardly felt desire for psychological integration, for bringing into harmony two worthy ideals in one's life that seem mutually inconsistent. Sometimes it is expressed in an inwardly felt desire for community, or mutually enhanced relations with others. And sometimes it is expressed as an inwardly felt desire for freedom from inordinate attachment to things finite, letting go into an infinite and wider whole. These three forms of satisfaction—of lived beauty—are found in religions and represent what might be called three general forms of salvation, experienced in their subjective dimensions: salvation through integration, salvation through communion, and salvation through letting go. Often, the three go together.

DELIGHT IN DIVERSITY

It is my hope that what we have discussed has helped you understand a process approach to world religions. It involves sensitivity to four faces of the sacred: the Abyss, the All, the Divine, and the Present Moment. It involves recognizing that the divine can itself be experienced in one or some combination of several ways: as One-embracing-many, One-within-many, and One-between-many. It involves an awareness that the many world religions, even in their finitude, contain various truths, and that these truths can be embodied in truthful belief, truthful awareness, and truthful living. It involves recognizing that these truths can be acquired through two forms of learning: learning from mind-to-body and also from body-to-mind. It involves a recognition that, in the last analysis, the truths of the world's religions are in service to a deeper human aim, namely the realization of ways of experiencing that are harmonious and intense: that is, beautiful. And it involves a realization that peace, understood as a creative process of living in harmonious intensity with others and the world, is itself a supreme form of beauty toward which all humans are lured by God, relative to individual settings and circumstances. I wish to conclude this chapter with a final word about the role that delight in diversity must play in the minds and hearts of religious and non-religious people if they are to contribute to peace in the world and peace between religions.

Toward this end, let us recall Haldane's remark that, after years of observing nature, he could only conclude that God has an inordinate fondness for beetles. From a process perspective, this quip deserves a place in our personal canon of holy sayings, because it reminds us that God is not reducible to our understanding of God. It also reminds us that there may be dimensions of God that are known only to other creatures but not to humans. And it reminds us that what can seem strange and alien to us may well be loved and embraced by God in ways we will never and need never understand. Taken together, these three ideas have a single and radical implication. They rightly suggest that spirituality is measured not only by faith and hope and love but also by our capacity for delight in diversity.

By delight in diversity, I mean two things. First, I mean appreciation for unique ways of being in the world, embodied by human beings and other forms of life. In human life, these different ways of being are expressed in different cultures, different religions, different languages, different sexual orientations, different personality types, and different phases in the course of an individual life, ranging from the innocent joys of childhood to the wisdom that comes with age. There is not simply one way to be human in this world; there are many. In the course of a lifetime, if we are lucky, we get to participate in several different ways.

Ultimately, for the theist, this appreciation for different ways of being human is rooted in faith and an awareness that the worlds around us—and also the worlds within us—form a diverse whole that is filled with many different kinds of beings, with the many making the whole richer. This whole is the whole of human life and the whole of the planet and the whole of the universe, but it is also, still more deeply, the divine life, which includes all other things.

Perhaps Jews and Christians can celebrate God's appreciation for the diverse whole of creation by remembering the first creation story in Genesis, read in dialogue with Buddhism. On the seventh day of creation, God stopped working and simply enjoyed the beauty of the heavens and the earth, declaring the diverse whole of the universe very good. Process thought is deeply sensitive to the wisdom in this story. The divine reality is enriched, not depleted, by the variety in the universe. God would not be "God" were there not a multifaceted universe to be known and loved. And we would not be ourselves if we did not share in this divine delight in something other than us. Delight in diversity involves appreciation of the multiplicity of the world, without needing to reduce this multiplicity to "one thing" that serves human ends. From this awareness arises a creative and sometimes prophetic imagination that is sufficiently open to fresh possibilities for creative response to existing situations. This openness is at the heart of peace as described at the outset of this chapter, a peace that is adventurous rather than static, flexible rather than fixed, and that thereby poses a meaningful alternative to the intoxication of violence. Peace on earth requires not only the building of healthy communities but also a capacity for holy relaxation, for resting in pure delight at the manyness of the world—beetles and Buddhists included.

In addition to appreciation for the multiplicity of the universe, however, there is a second aspect to delight in diversity and it might best be called *empathy for the particular*. By this phrase I mean (1) a sensitivity to the individual thou-ness of individual living beings, especially to people and other animals with obvious capacities for suffering and joy, (2) an awareness that the being at issue is not simply an object for others but also a subject of its own life, worthy of moral regard as an individual, and (3) an intuitive sharing in the joys and sufferings of others, feeling their feelings. In a process context, this "feeling of feelings" is part of what makes God "God," and it can also be part of what makes us who we are. God's embrace is an ongoing and everlasting process of deep listening in which the divine reality shares in the joys and sufferings of all living beings, moment by moment, not unlike the way in which the celestial Bodhisattva Kuan-yin of Buddhism shares in their sufferings. She is the goddess of tears, and from a process perspective, the One-embracing-many is also a goddess of tears—and of joys, too. We become fully human not only by taking delight in the manyness of the universe but also through our capacity for deep listening and feeling the feelings of others.

For most of us, it is often easy to have this kind of empathy in relation to other people of like mind and spirit, such as friends and family members. Many people also have this kind of sensitivity in relation to individual animals, especially pets, who are subjects of their own lives in ways that enrich and widen human consciousness. But it is often more difficult to be sensitive to individual human beings, especially adults, who have different beliefs, attitudes, and practices. We tend to lump other individuals into categories such as "Jew" or "Muslim" or "Hindu" or "Christian" or "atheist" and then treat them as if they were statistics or generalities. Whitehead calls this tendency "the fallacy of misplaced concreteness" (PR 7, 18, 93, 94), because it confuses abstractions in the mind with living beings from whom those abstractions may or may not be drawn. In times of warfare, this fallacy is especially pronounced. We train young people to approach others as "enemies," as if the very word "enemy" offsets any blame or guilt on the part of the ones being trained or the trainers. Soldiers are trained to forget the fact that enemies are people and that their deaths occur one by one, forever affecting the lives of others who are left behind to mourn.

If violence in our world is to be minimized, the minimization can best occur through forms of education—formal and informal, religious and secular—that help people grow in their capacity for delight in diversity. One aspect of this delight is gratitude for the multiplicity of the world and another is empathy for individuals who suffer. A meaningful degree of peace on earth becomes a possibility for human beings only insofar as religious people and non-religious people become gifted in the arts of delight. I hope that, in some small way, the ideas in this book have contributed to these arts.

Conclusion

Gandhi and Whitehead

The most influential advocate of peace between religions during the past century was a Hindu: Mahatma Gandhi. Gandhi's hope for peace between religions was grounded in his conviction that all religions are inspired by an indwelling lure toward wisdom but that no single religion has all the wisdom relevant to salvation, however understood. He proposed that if there is to be peace between religions, people of one religion must undertake friendly readings of other religions, seeking the truth in the other religions, trusting that the truth of the other religions complements, rather than competes with, the truth of their own.

In many ways, a Whiteheadian or process approach to interreligious dialogue extends this Gandhian legacy. To purists, it may seem odd to mention Gandhi and Whitehead in the same breath, because at many levels the two men were very different. Whitehead was a British-turned-American philosopher whose public life was in the world of thought and whose intellectual vocation was to create peace—harmonious contrasts—between ideas, particularly ideas concerning religion and science, philosophy and art, psychology and biology, poetry and politics. By contrast, Gandhi was a spiritual seeker, deeply involved in political struggle, who sought peace between people, particularly Hindus and Muslims. Gandhi was more interested in how communities might live together, making the whole richer, than in how ideas might fit together. Nevertheless, these two men had similar convictions. They both thought that the deepest peace is inseparable from, and in some ways identical to, the very life of God; they both thought that the divine life operates in human life through persuasion rather than coercion; they both thought that Jesus of Nazareth—himself a prince of peace—exemplified this non-violent way of working in the world; and they both thought that Christians, as well as others, who think they have a monopoly on peace are mistaken.

Additionally, they both had what one contemporary science writer, Ursula Goodenough, in *The Sacred Depths of Nature*, calls a "covenant with mystery." They knew that ultimate truth is always more than anyone's concept of it and that people who claim to possess it are foolish. To repeat what Whitehead states in his preface to *Process and Reality*, "There remains the final reflection, how shallow, puny, and imperfect are attempts to sound the depths in the nature of things. In philosophical discussion the merest hint of dogmatic certainty as to finality of statement is an exhibition of folly" (PR xiv).

This is not to say that Whitehead and Gandhi would agree on all matters. Whitehead thought that the *depths in the nature of things* include more than the divine peace and divine lure toward wisdom. These depths include what Zen Buddhists call the self-structuring creativity of each present moment of human experience that allows human beings to do great good in the world as well as to inflict violence on one another. As Thomas Kasulis explains in his discussion of the Zen view of self in *Zen Action/Zen Person*, in each present moment "there is something more than mere determinacy from the past; there is also the present moment working in its own creative way... Experience... *structures itself*... Each moment is new. Each time is a 'first time.'"[1]

A recognition of this self-structuring creativity led Whitehead to ask a basic question: Is the self-structuring creativity of the universe identical with God or different from God? And if different from God, is God an expression of, or an exception to, this creativity?

He resolves this issue by speaking of the self-structuring creativity of finite beings as expressions of an ultimate reality he calls Creativity. He calls God the primordial expression of this Creativity, but not the only expression. In Whitehead's view, when the British soldiers killed Indian peasants as they protested British rule, they were exemplifying the freedom of Creativity, which is ultimate and irreducible in its way. However, they were not conforming to the will of God, which is likewise ultimate and irreducible. In this respect, Whitehead's own thought is Confucian. It sees the divine reality—heaven—as one expression of creativity, but it also sees earth and human beings as alternative expressions, sometimes conforming to and sometimes diverging from the heavenly mandate. This is one reason some speak of two ultimates—the ultimacy of the divine reality and the ultimacy of freedom—expressed in the self-structuring creativity of each present moment. This divine reality is the ultimate actuality of the universe, whereas freedom is the ultimate reality of the universe, of which even God is an expression. Stated differently, the divine reality is the One-embracing-many, and freedom is the dimensionless freedom of which the One and the many are expressions. In chapter 3, I spoke of this dimension, freedom as the Abyss. It is a source of horror in the world, but also of great beauty and diversity.

Can the religious people of our world, those whose very religions are among the many which are included within the One, freely accept their own diversity? In their freedom, can they participate in God's love of diversity?

In this book I argue that they—*we*—can indeed participate in that love, and that in its own way the philosophy of Whitehead can help us do this. More specifically, my proposal is that people of different religions and no religion can use Whitehead's thought as a philosophical companion for the study of world religions. Such study is an important aspect of helping create a culture of peace in our world. It can occur in the church or mosque, the synagogue or *sangha,* and also in the college or university. Of course, as this study occurs, it simultaneously involves interpreting Whitehead's own thought in light of the many religions. Not only can Whitehead can help us understand the world's religions; the world's religions can help us appreciate and understand Whitehead.

In order to demonstrate how Whitehead's thought might serve as a companion to such study, then, let us envision a college student who is reading a basic textbook on the world's religions while taking a course on Whitehead's *Process and Reality* and other works in the Whiteheadian tradition. For the sake of concreteness, let us imagine that she is a biology major and that she shares her newly found interest in the world religions with one of her biology professors, who, like J. B. S. Haldane whom I quoted in the previous chapter, is skeptical of religions. Her professor reminds her that religion is an activity within, not apart from, the evolutionary history of life on earth. She agrees with her professor, and reminds the professor that scientific methods and the insights of science must likewise be outcomes of evolution and forms of adaptation, subject to the laws of physics and chemistry and to the dynamics of natural selection. She says: "If scientific insights are not invalidated by the fact that they are outcomes of evolution, then neither should religious insights be invalidated." This recognition of the co-evolving nature of religion and science leads her to believe that religion and science are two modes of human activity, both of which can yield wisdom concerning the nature of reality. In her study of the many religions, then, I offer the following sampling of insights that seem "true" from a Whiteheadian point of view, and that she will come to appreciate as she proceeds in the course on world religions. For illustrative purposes, I consider only eight of the world's many religious traditions, trustful that readers might include others in lists of their own.

First, our hypothetical student would come to appreciate *Hindu insights* concerning the divine reality as personal *(Saguna Brahman)* and transpersonal *(Nirguna Brahman)* and the idea of a "continuing journey" after death until wholeness is realized. A Whiteheadian approach would see *Saguna Brahman* as the side of God that "feels the feelings" of all living beings (the consequent nature of God) and *Nirguna Brahman* as a name for the reservoir of pure potentiality (the primordial nature of God) beyond personal characteristics or as a name for the creative Abyss of which the primordial nature is an expression. The gods and goddesses of Hinduism might then be understood as diverse faces through which God is discerned, analogous to the colors of a prism through which divine light shines. Karma would be understood as a description of the fact that, in each moment of existence, a human being finds himself or herself in conditions (inner and outer) that are partly the result of personal decisions made in the past, but to which he or she can creatively respond in the present moment itself, thus helping bring about alternative destinies for the future. And the continuing journey would be understood as the journey of a soul toward what David Ray Griffin in his *Parapsychology, Philosophy, and Spirituality* calls "peaceable selves," which can be understood as absorption into the consequent nature of God with no semblance of individuality remaining, or as everlasting communion in which individuality is completed.

Second, she would come to appreciate *Buddhist insights* concerning the interconnectedness of all things; the impermanence of all things; the illusion of having a skin-encapsulated ego; and the ultimate reality of *sunyata* (emptiness). A Whiteheadian approach would understand these claims as referring to the fact that all beings are indeed present in all other beings, such that nothing exists all by itself; that the universe is, in Whitehead's words, "perpetually perishing" in its subjective immediacy, such that even the good things in life cannot be clung to forever; that human beings are themselves a series of experiences extending from birth (and perhaps before) to death (and perhaps after) in which the "subject" is identical with the act of experiencing itself and partly composed of the world that is experienced; and that the ultimate reality of the universe is a spontaneous or self-structuring creativity of which even God is an expression.

Third, she would come to value *Jain insights* concerning the intrinsic value of all life and the value of living non-violently in relation to life. Whiteheadians can understand this to mean that all living beings are subjects for themselves and not simply objects for others, and that their subjectivity deserves respect in its own right. A non-violent approach to animals as well as humans is a "truthful" relationship to them, which itself leads to a peaceful release from the violent aspects of acquisitive consciousness.

Fourth, she would be grateful for *Confucian insights* concerning the self as person-in-community who finds sacred value in family and community life; who lives in accordance with *li* or the connective patterns of the universe-in-process, as expressed in custom; who walks within the larger context of a trinity of heaven-earth-humanity. Whiteheadians can understand the trinity to refer to the whole of the universe as a seamless web of interdependent existence, with visible (earthly) and invisible (heavenly) dimensions; they can understand *li* to refer to the patterns of relationship that have emerged over time, creative conformity which helps people to live harmoniously with one another and become more fully human in the process; and they can understand the Confucian emphasis on family life as expressive of the fact that the divine part of the trinity is found in, not apart from, fidelity to the bonds of relationship on earth.

Fifth, she would be thankful for *Taoist insights* concerning divine presence as the Way of the universe itself, which can never be grasped but can always be trusted. Whiteheadians can understand this to name the divine reality as present in the universe in a continuous and ever-adaptive way as a directive and creative energy within human life and the whole of the cosmos. The "energy" of God would not be the physical energy of the universe per se, but rather the divine Eros itself, incarnationally present throughout the whole of life through divine subjective forms.

Sixth, she would come to appreciate *Islamic insights* concerning the unity of God who is both infinitely near *(tashbih)* and infinitely distant *(tanzih)* and who seeks the development of societies, not just individuals, that dwell in truthful sensitivity to the divine. Whiteheadians can understand this unity to refer to the all-inclusive spaciousness of the divine as it embraces the whole of existence; they can understand the distance to refer to the fact that God is always more than anyone's concept or experience of God, and they can understand the nearness to mean that God is within each living being as a lure toward wholeness. Following the lead of Muhammad Iqbal, who was himself influenced by Whitehead, they can understand Prophet Muhammad as a mouthpiece through whom divine aims for communal wholeness—for what Iqbal in 1934 called "spiritual democracy"—were revealed in the Qur'an. And again, following Iqbal, they can understand the vision of

Islam to include a recognition that humans need not be limited by ethnic and blood relations but can live free with a deeper sense of the spacious inclusiveness—the *tawhid*—of the divine, in cooperative relationship with a dynamic and evolving cosmos that is itself filled with divine energy.

Seventh, she would come to value *Jewish insights* concerning covenantal relations with God that are realized in fidelity to the bonds of relationship; the hallowing of everyday life through tradition and ritual; the reality of prophetic imagination; and the importance of the Sabbath as (in Abraham Heschel's words) the sacred in time. Whiteheadians can understand these covenantal relations as part of the give-and-take of divine human relations over time; they can understand the hallowing of life through tradition and ritual as a recognition that the whole of ordinary life can be a context for sacred awareness; they can understand the prophetic imagination as human attention to the indwelling lure of God as it presents contrasts between "what is and has been" and "what can be and should be," and they can understand the Sabbath as naming both a dimension of the divine life—the peace of the consequent nature—and a quality of human life in relationship that can be intentionally observed one day of the week, but felt and lived from in many days of the week.

Eighth, she would find herself grateful for *indigenous insights* concerning the kinship of all life and on invisible planes of existence with which harmony can be established. Whiteheadians can understand the kinship to refer to the fact that human beings are indeed biological and spiritual kin to other creatures, both because humans arise from biological evolution along with all other creatures and because they share with other creatures the reality of subjectivity. Indeed, Whiteheadians can be open to the possibility, recognized in many different indigenous traditions, that communication can occur between species through empathic conformity to the subjective states of others, humans and non-humans alike. And, along with indigenous traditions and numerous others, Whiteheadians will appreciate the possibility that there may be invisible beings (living ancestors, spirits, jinn, angels) who, if actual, are filled with subjective immediacy of their own unique kind. The latter possibility derives from the fact, emphasized by Whitehead, that three-dimensional space as discerned by the visual senses is but part of a larger space-time continuum (Whitehead called it the extensive continuum) in which other kinds of actualities might exist (PR 61–62).

Of course, these many insights are but a sampling. I do not include Christianity in this listing because I have offered an interpretation of Christianity in the first chapter. My point here though, is to illustrate how, in these and other ways, Whitehead assists in what Gandhi called "friendly readings" of the many world religions that can complement, but not replace, a more critical reading of the religions that is sensitive to the many ways in which they encourage unnecessary violence in the world. I conclude, then, with a final consideration of peace between religions.

I began this book by quoting Gandhi, whose hope for peace between religions was, and is, at the heart of the world's best hopes. One way to understand the Whiteheadian approach to world religions is to recognize that it builds upon and extends the Gandhian legacy in three important ways. An identification of these three ways helps summarize some of the most important proposals of this book.

First, the Whiteheadian approach envisions God—the primordial expression of universal creativity—as an indwelling lure toward wisdom within all living beings and within each human life, thus encouraging the view that each human being and each religion has something to teach the rest of the world. This does not mean that individual humans or the world's religions are earthen vessels of unadulterated wisdom. They can also be conduits for violence and tragedy and for what Marjorie Suchocki calls "original sin."[2] Accordingly, the religions require critical as well as sympathetic readings by their adherents and also by outsiders. But all religions contain wisdom that is inspired by the divine lure toward wisdom, and this wisdom is worth listening to and learning from. A Whiteheadian approach to peace between religions, like a Gandhian approach, emphasizes listening.

The second way in which a Whiteheadian approach extends a Gandhian approach is by envisioning this indwelling

lure of God as calling people to open themselves to wisdom
from unfamiliar sources, trusting that apparently incompatible
forms of wisdom can be gathered together and jointly affirmed
in the wider harmony of what Whitehead called "contrasts."
For Whitehead, a contrast is not a conflict. A contrast is the
kind of whole suggested by the yin-yang diagram of Chinese
philosophy, in which the black and white complete each other
by adding something not found in the other. Whitehead believed
that the whole of a person's life is a journey of creating and dis-
covering meaningful contrasts that add to the harmony and intensity of the person's life and that enrich his or her capacity to
add harmony and intensity to others' lives. We are on a journey,
says Whitehead, and the journey is never ending because there
are always new contrasts—new possibilities for beauty—to be
known and discovered (PR 24, 228).

A third way in which a Whiteheadian approach is Gandhian
is in its recognition of the limitations of language in expressing
human wisdom. In Western philosophy, it is sometimes assumed
that a person's wisdom is reducible to his or her verbalized "position," presented in an argumentative context, or to his or her
"values," objectified in a statement of well-argued beliefs. For
Whitehead, as for Gandhi, however, we humans can know more
than we say, and what we say is not always an exact replication
of what we know. Much of our knowing takes place in a deeper
and non-verbal dimension of our lives, in which we are aware of
ideas that have power and truth but that have not yet been ren-
dered into verbal formulation. Whitehead called these ideas
"lures for feeling," and he insisted that they are not reducible to
the language we use to express them (PR 25, 185–87, 224, 259,
273, 280). A Whiteheadian approach to peace between religions
will encourage people of one religion to listen for the pre-verbal
wisdom in people of another religion, some of which is better expressed in music or art or dance than in philosophy or theology.
We do a disservice to other religions if we focus only on what
they believe—stated in verbal texts as written and interpreted by
elites—without simultaneously attending to what they feel,
which may be where the wisdom truly lies.

As the decades of the twenty-first century unfold, it is important that we listen to the feelings of others, not only because we can learn from that wisdom but also because the future depends on it.

In the first chapter, I suggested that today many people face one or some combination of five challenges relative to our social locations and historical situations. It may help to repeat them here. They are:

The Compassion Challenge: that is, the challenge to identify resources within our traditions that are conducive to compassion—understood as respect and care for the community of life—and to live from these traditions in daily and community life.

The Repentance Challenge: that is, the challenge to acknowledge teachings and practices within our traditions that lend themselves to arrogance and violence, prejudice and ignorance, and to repent for them, adding new chapters to the ongoing histories of our traditions in a spirit of religious and cultural reconstruction.

The Simplicity Challenge: that is, the challenge to provide a meaningful alternative to what is arguably the dominant religion of our planet, namely consumerism, not only by lamenting the social and environmental costs of excessive consumption but also by showing that life can be lived frugally and joyfully without the tragedy of poverty and the trappings of affluence.

The Ecological Challenge: that is, to adopt an ecological outlook on life that acknowledges our biological and spiritual kinship with other creatures and that encourages building communities that are ecologically sustainable, that are compassionate toward other living beings, and that protect the earth's beauty for future generations, human and non-human alike.

The Diversity Challenge: that is, to appreciate religious and cultural diversity by respecting people of different religions and cultures, trusting that there are many valuable forms of religious and cultural expression and that all make the whole of life richer.

Most of this book has dealt with the final challenge, the Diversity Challenge. I have tried to show how people of different religions and no religion can welcome religious diversity. It may seem that this book's emphasis on listening to others—not only to what they say but also to what they feel—is aimed for the most part at cultivating that spirit of hospitality. But, in truth, a capacity for listening is necessary for responding to all of the challenges. We can flourish on our planet only if we learn to listen to the call of compassion, inviting us to seek resources for respect and care within our heritages; to the call of honesty, inviting us to acknowledge limitations within our traditions and to step forward by seeking new ways of thinking; to the call of frugality, beckoning us to live more simply so that others can simply live; and to the call of the earth, inviting us to accept our kinship with other creatures, for their sake and our own. From a Whiteheadian perspective, these various calls are really one call: the call of divine love as it beckons human beings to live compassionately and creatively. This call is also within the other creatures of our planet as an indwelling lure to live with satisfaction relative to the situation at hand. And it is within the universe as a whole as that lure toward complexity and consciousness, toward heightened capacities for creativity and feeling. To respond to this call is itself the great work of our time. Such a response involves deep listening. This listening is not passive or quiescent. It is among the most creative activities human beings can ever undertake. Insofar as the religions of the world encourage this listening, they have added to the very history of the earth, not by conquering it but by adding beauty to its poignant and gorgeous adventure.

Notes

Introduction

1. Diana Eck, *A New Religious America: How a Christian Country Became the World's Most Religiously Diverse Nation* (San Francisco: Harper SanFrancisco, 2001) 385.

2. See Sharon Daloz-Parks, *Big Questions, Worthy Dreams: Mentoring Young Adults in the Search for Meaning, Purpose and Faith* (San Francisco: Jossey-Bass, 2000) 23.

3. John Ruskin, *The Stones of Venice,* vol. 2 (New York: Garland Publishing, 1979) 145.

4. See the many references to this phrase in Alfred North Whitehead, *Process and Reality* (New York: The Free Press, 1978). Because I quote this text frequently, subsequent references to *Process and Reality* will be given in parentheses in the text with the abbreviation "PR" followed by page numbers.

Chapter 1: Let a Thousand Flowers Bloom

1. The sayings quoted here are taken from Margaret Chatterjee's landmark study, *Gandhi's Religious Thought* (New York: Macmillan Press, 1983).

2. *The Essential Gandhi: His Life, Work, and Ideas,* ed. Louis Fischer (New York: Randon House, 1983) 59.

3. Huston Smith, *The World's Religions* (San Francisco: Harper SanFrancisco, 1991).

4. David Dunn, "Nature, Sound Art, and the Sacred," in *The Book of Music and Nature,* ed. David Rothenberg and Marta Ulvaeus (Middletown, CN: Wesleyan University Press, 2001) 97.

5. Ibid., 97.

6. David Ray Griffin, *Parapsychology, Philosophy, and Spirituality: A Postmodern Exploration* (Albany, NY: State University of New York Press, 1997) 291.

7. Thich Nhat Hanh, "The Sun My Heart," in *Dharma Rain: Sources of Buddhist Environmentalism,* ed. Stephanie Kaza and Kenneth Kraft (London: Shambhala Press, 2000) 88.

8. John B. Cobb Jr., *God and the World* (Philadelphia: Westminster Press, 1976) 45.

9. See Joan Chittister, *Wisdom Distilled from the Daily: Living the Rule of Saint Benedict Today* (San Francisco: HarperCollins, 1991) 14–26.

10. Ibid., 14.

11. Alfred North Whitehead, *Adventures of Ideas* (New York: The Free Press, 1967) 155.

12. Ibid., 29.

13. Ibid., 346.

14. Chittister, *Wisdom Distilled,* 24.

15. See Paul Knitter, *Introducing Theologies of Religions* (Maryknoll, NY: Orbis Books, 2002). The four models are amply described throughout Knitter's book.

16. Thus is the Prophet Muhammad quoted in Muhammed Iqbal, "The Principle of Movement in the Structure of Islam," in *Liberal Islam: A Sourcebook,* ed. Charles Kurzman (New York: Oxford University Press, 1998) 259.

Chapter 2: A Walk in Beauty

1. Hans Küng. *Global Responsibility* (New York: Crossroads Publishing Company, 1991) vii.

2. From *The Earth Charter: Values and Principles for a Sustainable Future,* www.earthcharter.org [15 June 2004].

3. Alfred North Whitehead, *The Function of Reason* (Princeton, NJ: Princeton University Press, 1929) 8. See also the discussion of these three aims of life in Charles Birch and John B. Cobb Jr., *The Liberation of Life: From Cell to Community* (Cambridge: Cambridge University Press, 1981) 106.

4. Metta Sutra, "Loving-kindness," *Dharma Rain,* 29.

5. Brianne Swimme and Thomas Berry, *The Universe Story: From the Primordial Flaring Forth to the Ecozoic Era: A Celebration*

of the Unfolding of the Cosmos (San Francisco: HarperCollins, 1992) 243.

6. See PR, "feeling the feelings," 211; "subjective aims," 19, 27, 235, 275; "subjective forms," 16, 85–86, 88, 89, 141, 154, 155, 157, 168, 211, 226, 231–35, 249, 311; and "causal efficacy," 58, 64, 116, 168–83, 254.

7. See, for example, pp. 5, 6, 13, 27, and elsewhere in Gerald May's *Will and Spirit* (San Francisco: Harper SanFrancisco, 1982).

8. Charles Kimball, *When Religion Becomes Evil* (San Francisco: Harper SanFrancisco, 2002).

9. Marjorie Hewitt Suchocki, *The Fall to Violence: Original Sin in Relational Theology* (New York: Continuum, 1995) 16.

10. Griffin, *Parapsychology*, 291.

11. Ibid., 287–92.

Chapter 3: God's Fondness for Beetles

1. J. B. S. Haldane, quoted in G. E. Hutchison, *The American Naturalist* 93 (1959) 145–59.

2. Ursula Goodenough, *The Sacred Depths of Nature* (New York: Oxford University Press, 1998) 12.

3. Birch and Cobb, *Liberation of Life*, 152–53.

4. Mary Evelyn Tucker, "Ecological Themes in Taoism and Confucianism," in *Worldviews, Religion, and the Environment*, 221.

5. See Tu Weiming, "The Continuity of Being: Chinese Visions of Nature," in Richard C. Foltz, ed., *Worldviews, Religion, and the Environment: A Global Anthology* (Belmont, CA: Wadsworth, 2003) 210–11.

Conclusion

1. Thomas Kasulis, *Zen Action/Zen Person* (Honolulu: University Press of Hawaii, 1981) 139–41.

2. Suchocki, *The Fall to Violence*.

Index

Other Titles in the Faith Meets Faith Series

Toward a Universal Theology of Religion, Leonard Swidler, Editor
The Myth of Christian Uniqueness, John Hick and Paul F. Knitter, Editors
An Asian Theology of Liberation, Aloysius Pieris, S.J.
The Dialogical Imperative, David Lochhead
Love Meets Wisdom, Aloysius Pieris, S.J.
Many Paths, Eugene Hillman, C.S.Sp.
The Silence of God, Raimundo Panikkar
The Challenge of the Scriptures, Groupe de Recherches Islamo-Chrétien
The Meaning of Christ, John P. Keenan
Hindu-Christian Dialogue, Harold Coward, Editor
The Emptying God, John B. Cobb Jr. and Christopher Ives, Editors
Christianity Through Non-Christian Eyes, Paul J. Griffiths, Editor
Christian Uniqueness Reconsidered, Gavin D'Costa, Editor
Women Speaking, Women Listening, Maura O'Neill
Bursting the Bonds?, Leonard Swidler, Lewis John Eron, Gerard Sloyan, and Lester Dean, Editors
One Christ—Many Religions, Stanley J. Samartha
The New Universalism, David J. Kreiger
Jesus Christ at the Encounter of World Religions, Jacques Dupuis, S.J.
After Patriarchy, Paula M. Cooey, William R. Eakin, and Jay B. McDaniel, Editors
An Apology for Apologetics, Paul J. Griffiths
World Religions and Human Liberation, Dan Cohn-Sherbok, Editor
Uniqueness, Gabriel Moran
Leave the Temple, Felix Wilfred, Editor
The Buddha and the Christ, Leo D. Lefebure
The Divine Matrix, Joseph A. Bracken, S.J.
The Gospel of Mark: A Mahayana Reading, John P. Keenan
Revelation, History and the Dialogue of Religions, David A. Carpenter